UNION ON THE KING'S HIGHWAY

*THE
CAMPBELL-STONE
HERITAGE OF UNITY*

UNION ON THE KING'S HIGHWAY

*THE
CAMPBELL-STONE
HERITAGE OF UNITY*

Dean Mills

College Press Publishing Company, Joplin, Missouri

Table of Contents

PREFACE

The evangelical revival that swept the frontier in the early 1800's produced the origins of a group in Kentucky known as the Christians under the leadership of Barton W. Stone. During that same decade another group originated in Pennsylvania led by Thomas and Alexander Campbell, which later became known as Disciples or Reformers. Both groups came from Presbyterian backgrounds and placed emphasis upon the Scriptures as the only authoritative guide for the church and were advocates of Christian unity. As the influence of the two groups spread they became consciously aware of their similarities. Close contact among several of the preachers led to discussions in Kentucky in 1831 regarding the possibility of state-wide union which became a reality in 1832.

The first two chapters of this book will give a brief summary of the origin of the two groups with emphasis upon their concern for unity. While numerous histories are available with much of the information found in these two chapters it is deemed essential to give enough detailed background of the men and their followers to present the reader with the ideas and experiences that produced them and brought them to a position for union. The stage for the union will be set as their similarities and differences are presented in chapter three and the doctrines, experiences, and local unions prior to 1832 which served to draw them together are discussed in chapter four. Chapter five will give detailed information regarding the union in Kentucky, the method used to facilitate the union, and the success of the union within that state. The final two chapters are concerned with the border states of Kentucky with chapter six dedicated to the state of Ohio where considerable turmoil existed because of the union and chapter seven offering summary accounts of union in the other border states.

This book seeks to fill a three-fold need within the brotherhood of the Churches of Christ and Christian Churches. First, while all the general histories contain brief accounts of the Lexington meeting in 1832 and the union, no detailed study exists which gives a precise history of the event and the serious problems that developed which kept many of the Christian order from uniting, particuarly in Ohio and Indiana. It will aid in filling this information gap. A need also exists for those from this heritage to study in the ideas of these early leaders and recover the plea for unity that dominated the thinking of the pioneers of the movement. It is hoped that this book may provide a springboard for inquiring minds to begin re-studying the plea for unity that can be offered by our brotherhood. Finally, there is a need to study the attitudes surrounding the union: those which aided union and those which discouraged it. Right attitudes are essential if the appeal for unity presented by our brotherhood ever receives a hearing in the Christian arena.

Historical research involves scholarly and thorough investigation of primary and secondary source material. Much of the information contained in this dissertation comes from the publications of the era, including *The Christian Messenger, The Christian Baptist, The Millennial Harbinger, The Evangelist, The Gospel Advocate,* and the *Christian Palladium.* Some private journals were investigated, but only one, the journal of John Rogers, provided significant information. That which reflected this period of time was put together at a later date using news items he had written for the periodicals. Sometimes he added personal information which he was able to recall. Church records provided only a small amount of information because of the scanty presence of materials. The thinking that only the Bible should be the guide for the church was carried to the extreme that no written records should be kept, and few emerged from that era of time. The Disciples Historical Society has numerous files on churches that have existed from this time, but most of the information is of a later date.

Autobiographies and biographies provided a considerable amount of information and some interpretation of the events which proved quite helpful. Especially helpful were some of the state histories that provided the information for the final chapter.

Historical writing requires that the facts be presented truthfully and that some interpretation be made of those facts. It also requires that when new truth is discovered from the investigation that it be presented with complete support for conclusions that differ from what others have concluded. The careful reader will want to consult the footnotes at the end of the chapters for some new information pertinent to doctrinal development, but not considered significant for inclusion into the text.

The original spelling in the quotations has been retained without noting it in the text unless a word is misspelled in the typesetting process originally. Quotations from journals also are carried over exactly as recorded without changing abbreviated symbols and words.

DEFINITIONS

Since a few terms used may be new to certain readers, this brief glossary is offered to aid understanding.

Arianism
: The teaching that Christ was not the eternal son of God nor of the same substance.

Anti-Burgher Seceder
: In 1733 a branch of the Presbyterians in Scotland seceded from the main body, objecting to the right of lay landlords to appoint ministers instead of the parish. Later another division occurred over the issue of whether or not members could subscribe to an oath imposed legally upon any one who became a burgesses, creating the Burgher and Anti-Burgher split. Both groups sent missionaries into Ireland and Thomas Campbell was a

member of the Anti-Burgher Seceder sect.

Calvinism
A term applied to the five principle doctrines of John Calvin: (1) total depravity, (2) unconditional election, (3) limited atonement, (4) irrestible grace, and (5) perserverance of the saints.

Socinianism
Named after Faustus Socinus who denied the Trinity and believed that Jesus was not divine or he could not have died. He considered baptism a rite only for Jewish and pagan converts and those born of Christian parents had no need to be baptized.

Tunkers
Usually referred to as Dunkers, but get the name Tunkers from the German work, *tunken,* meaning "to dip." The group originated in Germany in 1708 and some of them emigrated to America in 1719 led by Peter Becker, and in a few years the entire membership came. They were congregational in church government, believed the Bible was the only rule of faith and practice for the church, baptized only adults (triune immersion) and opposed taking any kind of an oath.

1

BARTON W. STONE AND THE CHRISTIAN CHURCHES

INTRODUCTION

The Christian Church in Kentucky originated from the leadership provided by Barton W. Stone. Born in Maryland and educated in North Carolina at David Caldwell Academy, Stone moved to central Kentucky in 1796 where he was ordained two years later by the Transylvania Presbytery. He and four other Presbyterian ministers withdrew from the jurisdiction of the Synod of Lexington in 1803 and soon formed their own presbytery. It was dissolved in 1804 freeing Stone from any ecclesiastical organization or creed as he appealed to the Scriptures alone as the only authoritative guide for Christians and the basis for Christian unity.

Similar positions, independent of the Stone movement, developed under the leadership of James O'Kelly in Maryland, Virginia, and North Carolina; Elias Smith and Abner

Jones in New Hampshire. A rather informal union developed among these groups from sharing in conference meetings together and they became known as the Christian Connection.

FRONTIER RELIGION

Christianity faced a low tide on the frontier at the beginning of the nineteenth century in America. Numerous factors produced this low state that characterized the early American West. The opening of virgin lands brought the Easterners to the frontier with a desire for adventure and financial gain. They prepared the necessary supplies, loaded a few home furnishings and their families on wagons and moved westward, often leaving church affiliations behind.[1] When they arrived at their destinations, homes needed building, lands cleared, and crops planted; little time remained to devote to religion. Bishop Asbury, founder of the Methodist Episcopal Church, made a trip through Tennessee in the 1790's and, seeing the spiritual condition of the populace, made this entry into his journal: "When I reflect that not one in a hundred came here to get religion; but rather to get plenty of good land, I think it will be well if some or many do not eventually lose their souls."[2] The enticement of fortune also captured many of the preachers so that they devoted little time to their profession.[3]

Change in the state of religion came through revivals. James McGready, a Presbyterian minister in North Carolina, generated revivals wherever he preached. His main mission was directed toward the apathetic church members and the unconverted. Some antagonists accused him of diverting people from their work and "running people distracted."[4] His opponents visibly showed their contempt by burning his pulpit and writing him a threatening letter in blood.[5] Faced with such opposition he moved to Logan County, Kentucky in 1796.[6]

McGready ministered to three congregations in Logan County: Muddy River, Gasper River, and Red River. He soon encountered in these congregations the lethargic condition he had left in North Carolina. His eastern opponents had failed to convince him that his methods were wrong and he began using his revivalistic methods in Logan County. Small revivals erupted in 1797 and 1798, but soon died out.[7]

Success finally came for McGready in 1799 as he managed to keep the revival fervor at a peak. News of this small religious awakening spread to nearby areas with some positive effects. The congregations McGready served maintained their newly acquired awakened state into the next year. When he announced a "sacramental service" at Gasper River people came from several miles away to attend and hear McGready preach.[8] The crowd was too large for local accommodations and the suggestion of camping at the meeting met approval giving birth to the "camp meeting." The meeting lasted four days with both Methodists and Presbyterians taking part in the preaching. It met with such success that McGready scheduled similar services at other points in Logan County and kept the revival going. Others caught this spirit and the awakening spread to other areas of Kentucky and Tennessee. The news traveled into central Kentucky where one of McGready's past acquaintances from North Carolina, Barton W. Stone, heard of it.[9]

STONE'S EARLY LIFE AND WORK

Stone was born on December 24, 1772, near Port Tobacco, Maryland. Three years later his father died, leaving Mrs. Stone alone to raise seven sons and one daughter, and she moved them to Pittsylvania County, Virginia, where Barton was raised.[10] He wanted an education and after the Stone estate was settled, he took his share and enrolled in the David Caldwell Academy at Guilford, North Carolina, in February, 1790, with the intention of studying law. Most of the Presbyterian preachers in the Carolinas had studied at David Caldwell Academy. Caldwell was a Presbyterian preacher and a graduate of Princeton in 1761. Although he formed the entire faculty of the school it had gained a wide reputation of being an "Academy, a College, and a Theological School."[11] Needless to say, religion played a major role in the school's life.

When Stone entered the Academy, nearly thirty students had recently embraced religion under the preaching of James McGready. Stone observed this group and noticed that they differed from other religious advocates in that they were quite sincere. In this atmosphere he wrestled so continually with religious questions that he resolved to leave to get "away from the constant sight of religion." He soon changed his mind but resolved that theology was not going to interfere with his studies. He would pursue his schoolwork and let the religious-minded students go their way.[12]

Everything went smoothly for Stone until his roommate, Benjamin McReynolds, encouraged him to accompany him to a nearby community to hear McGready preach. McGready's zeal, earnestness, and persuasive power impressed Stone. Although Stone was not converted, the meeting did bear heavily on his mind.

> Shall I embrace religion or not? If I embrace religion, I must incur the displeasure of my dear relatives, lose the favor and company of my companions — become the object of their scorn and ridicule — relinquish all my plans and schemes for worldly honor, wealth and preferment, and bid a final adieu to all the pleasures in which I had lived, and hoped to live on earth. Are you willing to make this sacrifice to religion? No, no, was the answer of my heart.[13]

Continually bothered with the matter, he finally determined

to "see religion at the sacrifice of every earthly good. . . ."[14]

The doctrine of salvation as taught by McGready and others of the Presbyterian school maintained that man not only was totally depraved, but must wait upon God's Spirit to take the initiative in a conscious conversion. Stone earnestly labored for a year to obtain saving faith in this manner, but never could gain the experience he desired. In February, 1791, when he again heard McGready preach, he left the meeting thinking there was no hope for him.[15]

Stone literally became a wrecked individual, both physically and emotionally. He knew what he wanted, yet God seemed to withhold it from him. His anxiety increased to such a level that he found it necessary to leave the Academy for a brief time. On his return he had the opportunity to hear William Hodge, one of Caldwell's former students. Hodge succeeded where McGready had failed. As he preached on the love of God, Stone experienced joy in his "troubled breast." When Hodge completed his message, Stone retired to the woods with his Bible and while reading and praying, found the peace of mind for which he had diligently searched.[16]

The ministry now attracted Stone instead of the study of law. He had some reservations about the orthodox position of the Presbyterian Church on the Trinity, but still the Orange Presbytery licensed him to preach in 1796. After a brief, unsuccessful preaching tour into the lower section of North Carolina with Robert Foster (a young man who also had just received his license to preach), Stone again felt despair and believed he was unqualified for the ministry. Deciding to go to Florida where no one would know him, he had just begun to journey when an elderly lady at a church told him he was "acting the part of Jonah." She advised him to go West if he disliked lower North Carolina. Robert Foster, his young friend, was in the same congregation that evening and agreed to accompany him westward.[17] They went to Tennessee where two of Stone's classmates at the Academy persuaded him to go to Lexington, Kentucky. Arriving in the Lexington area he began supply preaching in the fall of 1796 for the Cane Ridge and Concord congregations.[18]

The possibility of ordination faced Stone when these congregations asked him, in 1798, to become their regular minister. Before he could do so the Transylvania Presbytery had to examine and ordain him. Some of Stone's beliefs did not concur with the positions of the Presbytery. He had experienced no special call to preach and questioned the concepts of conversion they favored. He considered a call to preach unnecessary and also held differing views of the Trinity than those found in the *Westminister Confession of Faith.* When the day for examination and ordination arrived, some of the members of the Presbytery knew of his different convictions. He wanted to be ordained, but he also wanted to be honest.[19] When his examiners asked, "Do you receive and adopt the *Confession of Faith,* as containing the system of doctrine taught in the Bible?," he replied, "I do, as far as I see it consistent with the Word of God."[20] No one objected to the response and the Presbytery ordained him on October 4, 1798.

THE CANE RIDGE REVIVAL

When news of McGready's revival reached Stone in 1800, he decided to visit his old acquaintance and observe the awakening personally. In early spring, 1801, he journeyed nearly 200 miles to Logan County.[21] He was quite impressed with what he observed and determined to try some of the same methods with his own people.

Stone's first efforts with these methods produced immediate results. As a consequence of his first sermon at Concord, two young girls were "struck down under the preaching of the Word, and in every respect exercised as those were in the south of Kentucky."[22] Returning to Cane Ridge the next day he found that his report of the revival, in addition to his sermon on the previous day, had created a religious fervor there. Several people in the community began searching for salvation and "some had found the Lord, and were rejoicing in Him." A group had gathered at Stone's house where within twenty minutes after his arrival "scores had fallen to the ground. . . ."[23] These were the first instances of revival techniques and responses in central Kentucky, and Stone is credited with bringing the revival to that sector of the state. From Concord and Cane Ridge it spread throughout many of the congregations in that region and into northern Kentucky, leading to the beginning of the camp meetings in central Kentucky.

The first camp meeting in that region occurred at the Concord church in June, 1801, at a sacramental service.[24] Nearly 4,000 people attended and camped on the grounds. Similar meetings were conducted at other congregations and the revival spirit prevailed. It reached its height at Cane Ridge in August, 1801, in a meeting that lasted a week. Estimates of attendance reached as high as 25,000[25] and an estimated 3,000 conversions were reported.[26] All classes of people attended, including the governor of the state of Kentucky.[27]

At the Cane Ridge revival, Baptist, Methodist, and Presbyterian preachers participated in the speaking with the Methodists and Presbyterians joining together in the communion service. One eyewitness reported:

> I attended with 18 Presbyterian ministers; the Baptist and Methodist preachers, I do not know how many; all being either preaching or exhorting the distressed with more harmony than could be expected.[28]

Denominational lines tended to fade in the revivals. But

this cooperative spirit had a short duration. Those unsym-
pathetic to the awakening emphasized their historic creeds
and confessions as they argued against the revivalistic
brethren.[29] A divisive spirit began to grow; a spirit that Stone
labeled "sect consciousness." This development eventually
convinced him that formal creeds kept Christians divided. He
later wrote, "My heart was sickened, and effectually turned
against such creeds as nuisances of religious society, and the
very bane of Christian union."[30]

Sides formed rapidly in the Presbyterian Church over the
revival issue and the battle flourished. Those opposing the
awakening presented three main arguments: (1) supporting
ministers of the revival allowed the uneducated and unor-
dained to preach, (2) the exercises which accompanied
revivals created uncouth and disorderly scenes, and (3) the
awakening's doctrine of salvation offered to all men directly
contradicted the church's Calvinistic position.[31]

THE BREAK FROM THE PRESBYTERIAN CHURCH

Three months after the Cane Ridge meeting, Richard
McNemar, one of the principal revival leaders and a member
of the Washington Presbytery, faced charges of holding views
contrary to the *Westminister Confession*. At Cincinnati,
Ohio, October 6-9, 1802, the presbytery examiners concluded that he held Arminian views regarding salvation.
However, no trial took place and they permitted him to
return to his preaching point at Turtle Creek. A second attempt was made by the firm Calvinists to bring him to trial at
the spring meeting of the presbytery, April 6-11, 1803, and
they also included John Thompson of the Springfield congregation. The revivalist preachers controlled this meeting
and defeated the attempt at prosecution.[32]

The case surfaced once more when the Synod of Lexington, to which the Washington Presbytery belonged, met in Lexington in September, 1803. An examination of the records of the Washington Presbytery revealed confused and irregular accounts of their action in dealing with this situation. Three principal matters troubled the committee which examined the book of the Washington Presbytery:

> (a) McNemar and Thompson had been charged with teaching Arminian doctrines, yet neither of them had been tried; (b) the presbytery had written into its minutes (even without a trial) its belief that McNemar's teachings were dangerous; and yet (c) it had let these men go on preaching while these charges were hanging over them.[33]

The Synod resolved to take up the committee report and on Thursday, September 8, 1803, passed a motion to "approbate the proceedings of the Presbytery of Washington in that part of their minutes which respects the examination of Mr. McNemar."[34] Then:

> On motion resolved that the Synod now take up and determine the question whether the Presbytery of Washington were in order in publishing to the churches under their care; that the doctrines Mr. McNemar held were of dangerous tendency, and contrary to the constitution of our church, — which question being Called for was carried in the affirmative.[35]

No further action followed on Thursday, but enough had occurred to show the other four revivalists, Stone, Thompson, Dunlevy, and Marshall, that they were a minority. Stone later stated that "it was plainly hinted to us, that we would not be forgotten by the Synod."[36]

The first question addressed on Friday at the meeting of the Synod was, "Were the Presbytery of Washington in order in making appointment for Mr. McNemar at the Same Session at which they had taken a vote of censure on some of his Tenets?"[37] When the vote was taken on the question, eleven of the twenty-eight eligible delegates abstained and it carried by four votes. The Synod then proceeded to censure the Washington Presbytery for its actions in the McNemar case and for permitting him to continue preaching.[38]

The charges against McNemar and Thompson were then considered on Saturday, and during a recess, the five revivalist preachers retired to a "private garden" where:

> After prayer for direction, and a free conversation, with a perfect unanimity we drew up a protest against the proceeding of the Synod in McNemar's case, and a declaration of our independence, and of our withdrawal from their jurisdiction, but not from their communion.[39]

This protest, presented to the Synod on Saturday, contained three reasons for their actions: (1) the account extracted from the Washington Presbytery minutes gave distorted accounts of McNemar's views and was intended to stop the revivalists; (2) they had the right, according to the *Confession of Faith,* to interpret the Scriptures for themselves, but the Synod appeared to be denying them this privilege; and (3) they held differing views on the doctrine of grace than stated in the *Confession* and would withdraw to alleviate the Synod from the disagreeable task of having to try them as well as relieving the petitioners from trial under a confession they could not conscientiously acknowledge.[40] The petitioners left the meeting and went to the home of a friend.

The Synod acted quickly to restore them. A committee was appointed consiting of James Welsh, Matthew Houston, David Rice, and Joseph Howe to meet with the revivalists for the purpose of reconciliation. The committee got only an agreement from them that they would negotiate by replying to written questions with written answers. A motion in Synod to accede to these proposals was defeated and another committee appointed for further dialogue with the revivalists to get them to state in writing their objections to the *Confession of Faith.* The revivalists would give no written reply and ultimately the Synod suspended them. The next action was to inform the churches where these men ministered and attempt to keep them under the jurisdiction of the Synod. A circular letter was drafted and representatives sent to each of the churches.[41] They failed, however, to keep the churches from sympathizing with their ministers.

Stone and his fellow revivalists reported their action to their people as soon as they returned home. Fully supported by them, they almost immediately established a separate presbytery, naming it Springfield Presbytery. Its creation was intended to show that the seceders did not renounce Presbyterianism. They even proposed to return to the fellowship of the Synod of Kentucky if it would recognize their new structure, but the proposal did not meet the Synod's approval.[42]

On January 31, 1804, the revivalists published a pamphlet written by Marshall, Stone, and Thompson entitled *An Abstract of an Apology for Renouncing the Jurisdiction of the Synod of Kentucky, Being a Compendious View of the Gospel and a Few Remarks on the Confession of Faith.* The Synod replied to this with a pamphlet entitled *Circular Letter* explaining the reasons behind their actions in the suspensions.[43]

When the Presbyterian General Assembly met in 1804, it appointed a committee to join with five men appointed by the Synod of Kentucky to make additional attempts to reconcile the seceders. They arranged a meeting and all attended except McNemar. The seceders presented four basic principles for healing the schism:

(1) The essential unity of all Christians, (2) sustaining that unity in prayer, (3) Christian liberty with unity based on "Christian charity and mutual forbearance," and (4) God's unobstructed sovereignty over His church recognized simply in prayer and fraternity.[44]

This attempt also ended in failure.

23

Faced with their own painful experience of separation, the subject of Christian unity became a serious topic for them. While their presbytery had grown to fifteen congregations, they recognized they were building institutional structures that would divide them from others. Meeting at Cane Ridge on June 28, 1804, they ended the Springfield Presbytery, dissolving it by a document entitled *The Last Will and Testament of the Springfield Presbytery.* The five seceders were joined in signing this by David Purviance, another minister who had joined them after publication of the *Apology.*[45] They made a strong appeal for the sovereign authority of the Bible, congregational autonomy, and Christian unity. *The Witnesses' Address* closed with an appeal for unity.

> We heartily unite with our Christian brethren of every name, in thanksgiving to God, for display of his goodness in the glorious work he is carrying on in our Western country, which we hope will terminate in the universal spread of the gospel, and the unity of the church.[46]

In this order the Christian Churches emerged in Kentucky and Ohio. The next decade was a period of trial as Thompson and Marshall returned to Presbyterianism and Dunlevy and McNemar united with the Shakers. These developments left only Stone of the original group. He traveled into Ohio and Indiana winning converts and establishing new congregations. The movement also grew in Kentucky and some able converts filled the gap left by the defection of his former companions. The most notable of these was John Rogers.

STONE'S VIEWS OF CHRISTIAN UNITY

Stone once commented that schemes for union could be divided under four heads; (1) book union, (2) head union,

(3) water union and (4) fire union. He explained that book union rested on certain written articles of faith to which all must subscribe, head union was based on human opinions, and water union was established by immersion. He saw no real hope of union upon any of these, but rather upon fire union; a union founded on the Holy Spirit and the spirit of truth.[47] A union of "members of the Body" required a life-giving substance flowing through them. The substance of life was the Holy Spirit.

> How vain are all human attempts to unite a bundle of twigs together, so as to make them grow and bear fruit! They must first be united with the living stock, and receive its sap, and spirit, before they can ever be united with each other. So must we be first united with Christ, and receive his spirit, before we can ever be in spirit united with one another. The members of the body cannot live unless by union with the head — nor can the members of the church live united, unless first united with Christ, the living head. His spirit is the bond of union. Men have devised many plans to unite christians — all are vain. There is but one effectual plan, which is, that all be united with Christ, and walk in him. Zion must be purged from dead members, before she can shine in union and glory.[48]

Stone's plan for union had, basically, four guiding principles. First of all, the Christians must "have the spirit of the Bible and of the name *Christian*." They must exhibit a true picture of love and unity to others in order to effect Christian union. If love and harmony did not exist among them they would lose their witness to others giving them no reason to believe their platform for unity would work.[49]

The second fundamental was focused on the Bible. It alone, with no creeds or confessions, must be the guide.[50] He believed that creeds and confessions interpreted the Bible for people and left no room for opinion. Abandonment of human writings stood as an essential to free inquiry into the Scriptures. He contended that man-made creeds have always divided Christians and stood in the way of union and the only platform on which Christians could meet was the Bible.

As man-made creeds have always divided Christians and stood in the way of union — these must all be abandoned, and the Bible alone received as the only foundation and rule of faith and practice. On no other platform can all Christians meet.[51]

The third principle of union that Stone championed was the need to use Biblical terms and terminology. He believed that all sectarian labels must give way to the name "Christian" since he could not foresee people uniting on one of the names by which the different parties are distinguished.[52]

Biblical terminology must likewise prevail as the only vocabulary for the church. He contended this would eliminate many differences over unessential matters. He admonished his followers to confine themselves "to the language of the Bible as much as possible. Speculations are unprofitable, and injurious to the growth of vital piety and stand in the way of Christian Union."[53]

The right of private opinion, properly circumscribed, was another fundamental for Stone. On this issue he appealed to his understanding of the situation as it existed in the apostolic church.

In those days there were but a few terms of communion among Christians. All were admitted to fellowship who believed in the Lord Jesus Christ, and obeyed him; and their obedience was considered the best evidence of their faith. This was the lesson taught them by their Lord; who said, "By their works ye shall know them;" and "Whoso doeth the will of my Father, the same is my brother, my sister and my mother." If opinions of truth were to be made terms of fellowship, it is much questioned whether any two men on earth could so perfectly agree in all points, as ever to unite; there could be no union or fellowship on earth.[54]

Stone would not tolerate any private opinions that denied the Father, the Sonship of Jesus, His death, burial, and resurrection. Scripture, he believed, clearly taught these truths.[55] On the other hand, the greatest freedom was to be allowed to draw human deductions based on Biblical truth from the Word. Stone believed this area, where the sects battled, was the principal area that kept Christians separated. The fact that his followers held different opinions drawn from what they believed to be Biblical truth did not bother him.

> We do not wish to conceal from the world that there are Calvinists and Arminians in many doctrines in our communion, and yet we live in the closest bonds of Christian union. In this we rather glory; because we see the practicability of Christians living together in love and union, who differ in opinions.[56]

Evangelization of the world, Stone concluded, could never occur until Christians united as "one grand army" to enlist in the battle. This was his purpose in promoting union and he believed that every Christian who wanted to see the world evangelized under the Christian banner should labor diligently for the same cause. He believed that the party spirit stood "in direct opposition to the will of God, to the prayer of Jesus, and to the salvation of the world."[57] In the first issue of *The Christian Messenger* he wrote, "How soon would the world, seeing all Christians united, believe and be saved."[58] For this reason Christian unity became his "polar star."[59]

THE CHRISTIAN CONNECTION

Barton W. Stone held no original claim nor alone possessed the position of reformation on the basis of the Bible alone. Two other groups, one led by James O'Kelly and the other by Abner Jones and Elias Smith, had quite similar origins. These groups are important to the extent that they formed, with Stone's group, a body called the Christian Connection, or sometimes referred to as the "Christian Denomination." Following the merger of some of the followers of Stone and

27

Campbell, certain members of this group stood as the principal opponents to such a union and, therefore, must be included as important to this history.

James O'Kelly led a revolting segment of ministers in the Methodist Episcopal Church in 1792 in the region of Maryland, Virginia and North Carolina.[60] Ordained by Thomas Coke in 1784, he soon gained a reputation as a preacher of power and influence. He and some other ministers objected to the power of Bishop Asbury, especially in reference to the appointment of preachers. When the conference met in Baltimore in 1792, O'Kelly offered this resolution:

> After the bishop appoints the preachers at Conference to their several circuits, if any one thinks himself injured by appointment, he shall have the liberty to appeal to the Conference, and state his objection, and if the Conference approve his objection, the bishop shall appoint him to another circuit.[61]

Following a period of debate the resolution was divided into two parts. First, "Shall the Bishop appoint the preachers to the circuits?" and second, "Shall a preacher be allowed to appeal?"[62] The right of appeal failed and O'Kelly and nineteen fellow ministers withdrew from the conference and their churches followed their actions.[63] Methodist doctrine was not the issue and the O'Kelly group continued in Methodist principles except for church government. One of the prominent Methodist preachers of the day, Peter Cartwright, accused O'Kelly of withdrawing because he did not get to be the bishop. They called themselves Republican Methodists until the name was changed in 1794 at a meeting in Surry County, Virginia, where the ministers met to adopt some specific plans for the group. During the discussions regarding a name, Rice Haggard stood with a New Testament in his hand and said,

> Brethren, this is a sufficient rule of faith and practice, and by it we are told that the disciples were called Christians, and I move that

henceforth and forever the followers of Christ be known as simply.[64]

The motion received unanimous approval and the name "Christian" was adopted. The doctrines, however, remained Methodist in nature, except they had forsaken creeds, advocated the Bible alone as their only guide and took the name of Christian.

The other group with similar origins began in 1801 in Vermont and New Hampshire.[65] Elias Smith gathered about a dozen people together in September, 1801, in Lyndon, Vermont, and formed a church, taking also the name Christian and

. . . rejecting all party and sectional names, and leaving each other free to cherish such speculative views of theology as the Scriptures might plainly seem to teach them. This was probably the first FREE CHRISTIAN Church ever established in New England.[66]

The other principal worker in this area was Abner Jones, a Baptist preacher who became disenchanted with the ministry and left the Baptist Church in 1801. He and some others met at Sanborton in 1802 and organized "The Christian Conference." He went to Portsmouth, New Hampshire, and organized a "Church of Christ" in that community in 1803.[67] Jones considered himself free to preach anywhere and became an itinerant preacher, going anywhere he received an invitation. He felt a need, however, for ordination, and having no one to perform this, he turned to the Free-will Baptists. He was careful to inform them that he would not be bound by their peculiar beliefs, and at his ordination on November 30, 1802, said,

I will not acknowledge any of the devil's impositions. Understand me perfectly, brethren, I do not wish to join the Free-will Baptists. I wish Christian fellowship. If hereafter it should be asked, "Have you joined the Free-will Baptists?" the answer will always be "No." It shall not be said thereafter, "Brother Jones, you belong with us, and our rules are thus and so." I will never be subject to one of your rules; but if you will give me the right hand as a brother and let me remain a free man, just as I am, I should be glad.[68]

Smith and Jones worked together, but Jones would never join the Christian Conference because the founders wrote a set of articles of faith to which he would not subscribe. This resulted in the church at Portsmouth laying these aside and in 1805 the Conference followed this action, declaring that "the New Testament was the only and all-sufficient rule for Christians,"[69] thus removing the barrier of fellowship between the two groups.

Through fellowship of the ministers, religious periodicals, and conferences, the relationship grew among the three separate bodies; the Christians of Kentucky, the Christians of Virginia and North Carolina, and the Christian Conference of Vermont and New Hampshire. Each group had a conference by 1814 for the purpose of fellowship.[70] The conference meetings began being attended by those from the other conferences and this fellowship led to an informal union of these groups. J.F. Burnett later wrote:

> There is no available evidence of any definite time, nor any particular place, when and where the three separate bodies of the Christians came together and formed what is known as the Christian Church. Indeed, it is exceedingly doubtful that they ever were amalgamated in any formal, or technical way. All evidence points rather that they became acquainted with each other through correspondence and ministers traveling from one section to another in quest of souls for the kingdom.[71]

The flowing together of these three groups is remarkable. No committees or delegates met to organize a plan, no congregations made overtures toward others; it just occurred by mutual consent as each recognized the other as "brothers." Undoubtedly the key element centered in the matter of fellowship and for all three groups the only test of fellowship was Christian character.

This informal union demonstrated the practicality and possibilities of Christian unity on the basis of the Bible alone. After Stone began publishing *The Christian Messenger* in 1826, letters from different sections of the country from those who were representative of each of these groups reported the progress of the churches, announced various meetings and extended invitations for preachers to visit and proclaim the Word.

CHAPTER SUMMARY

Barton W. Stone, influenced by James McGready's revival methods, brought revival to central Kentucky resulting in the great Cane Ridge Revival. The revivalistic methods countered accepted doctrine within the Presbyterian Church and led to Stone's ultimate split with Presbyterianism. Christian unity became a serious issue to Stone at that time. He and some other ministers formed the Springfield Presbytery but soon recognized that even their own creation hindered Christian unity and they officially dissolved it with a document entitled *The Last Will and Testament of the Springfield Presbytery*. Stone continued to develop his ideas and formed a loose union with other groups who possessed similar thoughts on the Scriptures and the independent nature of the church. He began publishing *The Christian Messenger* in 1826 giving him opportunity to express his views to a wider audience.

---

1. This was not always the case. Among the Baptists some entire congregations moved from Virginia into Kentucky. Walter Brownlow Posey, *The Baptist Church in the Lower Mississippi Valley, 1776-1845* (Lexington: University of Kentucky Press, 1957), p. 5.

2. Walter Brownlow Posey, *The Presbyterian Church in the Old Southwest, 1778-1838* (Richmond: John Knox Press, 1952), pp. 22-23. Quoted from *The Jour-*

nal of Rev. Francis Asbury, Volume II (New York, 1852), p. 342.

3. *Ibid,* p. 22.

4. Catherine Cleveland, *The Great Revival in the West, 1797-1805* (Gloucester: Peter Smith, 1959), p. 39.

5. *Ibid.*

6. James DeForest Murch, *Christians Only* (Cincinnati: The Standard Publishing Company, 1962), p. 27.

7. Cleveland, p. 41.

8. Kenneth Scott Latourette, *A History of the Expansion of Christianity,* Volume IV (New York: Harper and Brothers Publishers, 1941), p. 192.

9. Posey, *The Presbyterian Church in the Old Southwest,* p. 24. Catherine Cleveland points out that overnight meetings had been conducted previously where people camped one night. But the Gasper River meeting received credit for being the first where they stayed for several days.

10. Murch, p. 83.

11. William Garrett West, *Barton Warren Stone: Early American Advocate of Christian Unity* (Nashville: The Disciples of Christ Historical Society, 1954), p. 3.

12. John Rogers, *The Biography of Elder Barton Warren Stone, Written by Himself, With Additions and Reflections* (Cincinnati: J.A. and O.P. James, 1847), Fifth edition, p. 7.

13. *Ibid,* p. 8.

14. *Ibid,* p. 9.

15. West, pp. 10-11.

16. *Ibid,* pp.11-12.

17. Rogers, *Biography of Stone,* p. 17.

18. West, p. 16.

19. *Ibid,* p. 17.

20. Rogers, *Biography of Stone,* p. 30.

21. *Ibid,* p. 34.

22. *Ibid,* p. 36.

23. *Ibid,* pp. 36-37.

24. Cleveland, p. 74.

25. *Ibid,* p. 75.

26. James R. Rogers, *The Cane Ridge Meeting-House* (Cincinnati: The Standard Publishing Company, 1910), p. 59.

27. Cleveland, p. 79. This is a quotation from a letter from a Presbyterian preacher, John Evans Finley, dated September 20, 1801, printed in the *New York Missionary* magazine in 1802.

28. *Ibid.* See also Rogers, *Biography of Stone,* pp. 37-38.

29. Charles C. Ware, *B.W. Stone* (St. Louis: The Bethany Press, 1932), p. 126.

30. Rogers, *Biography of Stone,* p. 48.

31. Winfred Garrison and Alfred DeGroot, *The Disciples of Christ, A History* (St. Louis: Christian Board of Publication, 1948), p. 102.

32. Ware, *B.W. Stone,* pp. 129-131. Accounts of this can be found in several good general histories. James Kemper led the opposition against the revivalists.

33. Garrison and DeGroot, p. 103.

34. William Warren Sweet, *Religion on the American Frontier: The Presbyterians, 1783-1840,* Volume II (New York: Cooper Square Publishers, Inc., 1964), p. 316.

35. *Ibid.*

36. Rogers, *Biography of Stone*, p. 47.

37. Sweet, *The Presbyterians*, p. 316.

38. *Ibid*, pp. 316-317.

39. Rogers, *Biography of Stone*, p. 47.

40. Sweet, *The Presbyterians*, pp. 318-319.

41. *Ibid*, pp. 320-323.

42. Garrison and DeGroot, p. 106.

43. W.W. Sweet, *Religion in the Development of American Culture, 1765-1840* (New York: Charles Scribner's Sons, 1952), p. 221. Most of the histories do not say anything regarding the *Circular Letter* published in response to the seceders.

44. Ware, *B.W. Stone*, p. 145.

45. A copy of both the *Will* and *The Witnesses' Address* which was appended to the *Will* can be found in Charles A. Young, *Historical Documents Advocating Christian Union* (Chicago: The Christian Century Co., 1904) pp. 19-26.

46. *Ibid*, p. 26.

47. Barton W. Stone, "The Retrospect," *The Christian Messenger*, Volume VII (October, 1833), pp. 314-316.

48. *Ibid*, p. 316.

49. Barton W. Stone, "Christian Union," *The Christian Messenger*, Volume II (December, 1828), p. 39.

50. Barton W. Stone, (no heading), *The Christian Messenger*, Volume IV (August, 1830), p. 202.

51. James M. Mathes, *Works of Elder B.W. Stone* (Cincinnati: Moore, Wilstach, Keys & Co., 1849) Second edition, p. 315.

52. *Ibid*, p. 314.

53. Barton W. Stone, "To the Public Teachers Who Are Called Christians," *The Christian Messenger*, Volume VI (July, 1832), p. 200.

54. Barton W. Stone, "Objections to Christian Union Calmly Considered," *The Christian Messenger*, Volume I (December, 1826), p. 27.

55. *Ibid*, p. 28.

56. Mathes, *B.W. Stone*, p. 50.

57. Barton W. Stone, "An Humble Address to the Various Denominations of Christians in American," *The Christian Messenger*, Volume II (November, 1827), p. 3.

58. Barton W. Stone, *The Christian Messenger*, Volume I (November 25, 1826), p. 5. This was the lead article in this issue and had no heading.

59. J.F. Burnett, *Rev. B.W. Stone: Did He Join the Disciples of Christ?* (Dayton: The Christian Publishing Association, n.d.), p. 16.

60. Murch, p. 32.

61. J.F. Burnett, *Rev. James O'Kelly; A Champion of Religious Liberty*, Booklet Two (Dayton: The Christian Publishing Association, n.d.), p. 12.

62. *Ibid*.

63. *Ibid*, p. 14.

64. *Ibid*, p. 16.

65. Murch, p. 32.

66. J.F. Burnett, *Rev. Abner Jones: A Man Who Believed and Served*, Booklet Three (Dayton: The Christian Publishing Association, n.d.), p. 13.

67. *Ibid*.

68. J.F. Burnett, *Elias Smith: Reformer, Preacher, Journalist, Doctor and*

Horace Mann: Christian Statesman and Educator, Booklet Five (Dayton: The Christian Publishing Association, n.d.), pp. 16-18.

69. *Ibid,* p. 19.

70. J.F. Burnett, *The Origin and Principles of the Christians, Booklet One* (Dayton: The Christian Publishing Association, n.d.), p. 45.

71. *Ibid,* pp. 45-46.

2

THE WORK OF THE CAMPBELLS

INTRODUCTION

Thomas Campbell came to America in 1807 from Ireland where he had labored to heal some unnecessary divisions existing in the Irish Presbyterian Church. He found similar divisions within Presbyterianism in America and soon came in conflict with the leadership within the Presbytery. Censured by them for permitting people not of their particular order to partake the Lord's Supper, Campbell found himself with no place to preach. He severed all ties with the Presbyterians in 1808-1809 and turned to the Scriptures as his only authority. He successfully gathered others around him and formed them into an association. Christian unity became a major concern for this group, leading to Campbell writing the *Declaration and Address* in 1809 designed to encourage and promote Christian unity. When his son Alexander arrived in 1809 and heard the principles his father had set forth he determined to commit his life to spreading them. Alexander emerged as the main leader of this group through the influence of his writing, debating, and preaching.

THOMAS CAMPBELL AND
THE *DECLARATION AND ADDRESS*

The party spirit that Barton Warren Stone faced in Kentucky in his efforts to promote Christian principles was not limited to that region of the world. Thomas Campbell came to the United States from Ireland in 1807 from a Presbyterian background in Ireland where divisions over issues in Scotland divided the Presbyterians in Northern Ireland, even though the issues were totally related to the political situations in Scotland and had no bearing on them. He made efforts to bring unity between some of these Presbyterian parties at the General Associate Synod in Scotland in 1806, but his pleas were ignored.[1] Campbell had been commissioned in 1804 by the Anti-Burgher Synod of Ulster as a delegate to the General Assembly in Scotland "with special reference to the consummation of an union between these branches of Presbyterians, called Burgher and Anti-Burghers."[2] He appealed to the Assembly on the basis that the Burgher oath was never required in Ireland and nothing existed to justify the extension of the division to the Presbyterian bodies in that land. Four years later, Alexander Campbell, the son of Thomas, met a gentleman while studying at Glasgow who had attended the meeting. Upon learning the relationship of the two Campbells he said:

> I listened to your father in our General Assembly in this city, pleading for a union between the Burghers and Anti-Burghers. But, sir, while in my opinion, he clearly out-argued them, they out-voted him.[3]

36

This defeat did not daunt Thomas Campbell's efforts for union. Returning to his home in County Antrim he continued his efforts for better relationships, but discovered individuals with a strong party spirit on both sides. He had contact with a group of Independents at Rich Hill who advocated the independence of the local congregation and the right of private opinion. These people influenced his thinking. Seeking a remedy for the problem of division, he gradually concluded that the Bible alone was "all-sufficient and alone sufficient" as a guide for the church. He "attempted sundry reforms, but was more or less prevented in all these by Synodical and Presbyterial interference and apathy."[4] These frustrations apparently were a factor in Campbell becoming ill, which led to his doctor's advice to take a sea voyage and get some rest. This led to his decision to come to the United States.

Thomas Campbell arrived in Philadelphia in May, 1807, where the Anti-Burgher Synod was then in session. He presented his credential and received assignment to the Presbytery of Chartiers in Western Pennsylvania.[6] When the Presbytery sent Campbell on a missionary tour to administer the Lord's Supper to Anti-Burgher Presbyterians scattered throughout the area, he found members of other Presbyterian bodies who had not participated in this rite for several years. Campbell knew that the Synod had passed an act in 1796 prohibiting communion, even on an "occasional" basis, with digressive Presbyterian groups.[7] Overwhelmed with compassion for these people, he decided to leave the matter of communing to the individual. He visited a few Anti-Burghers at Cannamaugh on the Allegheny River near Pittsburgh, taking William Wilson, a young minister, with him. After Campbell delivered the sermon of preparation for communion, commonly called "fencing the table," he expressed a regret at the numerous divisions which kept Christians separated and suggested that all present who felt in their own souls that they were Christians might participate, regardless of their

Synodical affiliations.[8]

Such notions were unacceptable to his young colleague and at the next meeting of the Presbytery of Chartiers on October 27-29, 1809, Wilson presented several charges of heresy against Campbell.[9] After listening to testimony from both sides the Presbytery censured and suspended Campbell, who then appealed to the Synod. That body reviewed the records and found "irregularities" in the action that had been taken.[10] While the Synod upheld the censure because of its dislike of Campbell's practices, it did not uphold the suspension. He returned to Western Pennsylvania, but he received no preaching appointments from his Presbytery. Nearly a year later, on September 14, 1808, Campbell gave notice that he was severing all ministerial connections with the Associate Synod and its subordinate bodies.[11] Eight months later, on May 23, 1809, the relationship formally ended.

The preaching of Campbell had not been without fruit. He gained the personal friendship of numerous individuals in Washington and Allegheny Counties who shared his convictions in his pleas for Christian liberty and union. Whenever Campbell spoke, a number of these individuals came to listen.[12] Since all the Associate Synod's congregations prohibited his speaking in their buildings, he conducted meetings in private houses and sometimes, during the summer, in shaded groves.[13] His primary theme in these meetings was the unity of all Christians on the basis of the Bible alone.[14]

The concept of the Bible as the only guide for Christians had occupied the thinking of Campbell for some time. Before he came to the United States he framed objections to the

> . . . assumption of any formula of religious theory or opinions, as the foundation of the Church of Christ; alleging that the holy Scriptures, Divinely inspired, were all-sufficient and for all the purposes contemplated by their Author. . . .[15]

Freed now from the restraints of a Presbyterian structure, he began to emphasize this view. Those who listened accepted his teaching so well that a need arose to establish some type of organization.[16]

Campbell decided to call his followers together to determine what course should be pursued. Accordingly, he announced a meeting, probably in the early summer of 1809, at the home of Abraham Altars, who lived between Mount Pleasant and Washington, Pennsylvania.[17] At the meeting Campbell first talked of the group's emergence and present situation, then began

> . . . to dwell with unusual force upon the manifold evils resulting from the divisions in religious society — divisions which, he urged, were as unnecessary as they were injurious, since God had provided, in his sacred Word, an infallible standard, which was all sufficient and alone sufficient, as a basis of union and Christian co-operation. He showed, however, that men had not been satisfied with its teachings, but had gone outside the Bible, to frame for themselves religious theories, opinions and speculations, which were the real occasions of the unhappy controversies and strifes which had so long desolated the religious world. He, therefore, insisted with great earnestness upon a return to the simple teachings of the Scriptures, and upon the entire abandonment of everything in religion for which there could not be produced a Divine warrant. Finally, after having again and again reviewed the ground they occupied in the reformation which they felt it their duty to urge upon religious society, he went on to announce, in the most simple and emphatic terms, the great principle or rule upon which he understood they were then acting, and upon which, he trusted, they would continue to act, consistently and perseveringly to the end. "That rule, my highly respected hearers," said he in conclusion, "is this, that WHERE THE SCRIPTURES SPEAK, WE SPEAK; AND WHERE THE SCRIPTURES ARE SILENT, WE ARE SILENT."[18]

The enunciation of such a rule did not escape criticism. Hope abounded that this day would mark the beginning of the end of religious divisions and that Campbell's small band would be the nucleus of a movement which would effect this. But even at this first meeting exception was taken to this newly-proclaimed rule. During the questioning period, one of the men, Andrew Munro, remarked that this principle would mean the end of infant baptism. Since this was a dear subject to Presbyterians, many others were aroused. Campbell replied, "Of course if infant baptism be not found in Scripture, we can have nothing to do with it."[19] This led to an exchange between two other attenders, Thomas Acheson and James Foster. Acheson responded to Campbell's reply by arising, walking off a short distance, laying his hand over his heart, and saying, "I hope I may never see the day when my heart will renounce that blessed saying of the Scripture, 'Suffer little children to come unto me, and forbid them not, for of such is the kingdom of Heaven.' "[20] Foster, who had arrived at decided Baptist views on the subject, replied, "Mr. Acheson, I would remark that in the portion of Scripture you have quoted *there is no reference, whatever,* to infant baptism."[21] Acheson left the meeting without a reply. Nevertheless, as far as is known, the rest of Campbell's followers remained for the rest of the meeting and, with the exception of Acheson, adopted his rule "with apparent unanimity, no valid objection being urged against it."[22] Although many historians date the launching of Campbell's movement to a later time, it seems more logical to date it with this meeting and the adoption of this rule which became a vital part of the group's attitude and thinking.

While Acheson seems to have been the only opponent at the meeting, others surfaced. Wide repercussions followed the adoption of this rule and numerous individuals refused to attend subsequent meetings.[23] Much of the discussion among the dissidents centered on the question of infant baptism. Campbell, at this point in time, believed in infant baptism, but thought that for the sake of peace and harmony and the cause of Christian union, it should be left to the chapter of non-essentials, leaving freedom to each individual to judge for himself on the subject.[24]

Promotion of Christian unity became the nerve of the

group and several recognized the need for more organization if this objective was realized. At a meeting at the head of Buffalo Creek on August 17, 1809, they resolved to form into an association under the title of "The Christian Association of Washington." They subsequently appointed twenty-one individuals to confer with Campbell on the best means of promoting Christian unity.[25] The need also existed for a meeting place, since homes did not provide them with adequate space and seating arrangements. This led to several in the neighborhood erecting a log building on the Sinclair farm located on the Mount Pleasant to Washington Road about three miles from Mount Pleasant.[26]

The committee settled on publication of the principles and aims of the association as the means to promote Christian unity. Accordingly, Campbell began writing a paper designed to inform the public at large of the purposes and intentions of the association. This document, known as the *Declaration and Address,* was read, unanimously adopted, and approved for printing on September 7, 1809.[27] In printed form it was fifty-six pages long and divided into four sections which one historian has summarized as follows:

> (1) *The Declaration* stating briefly the reasons for the organization of the Christian Association of Washington and proposing a tentative constitution; (2) the *Address,* setting forth in logical form the principles of Christian unity and the means by which it might be attained; (3) the *Appendix* in which certain points in the *Address* are amplified and possible criticisms are answered; and (4) a *Postscript* suggesting steps that should be taken for the promotion of the crusade.[28]

While Thomas Campbell busied himself with the *Declaration and Address,* his wife, Jane, and their seven children sailed to the United States. She had attempted the jouney in October, 1808, but a severe gale damaged the ship which halted the voyage. The family went to Glasgow, Scotland, where her son, Alexander, studied in the university. They left

Scotland on August 3, 1809, and arrived in New York on September 29. As they traveled toward Washington, Pennsylvania, Thomas set out from there to meet them, and on October 5, 1809, the Campbell family was re-united.[29] During the next three days of travel to Washington, Thomas shared with his family his experiences and frustrations in the United States. As he spoke of his withdrawal from the Anti-Burgher Presbyterians, his son, Alexander, was surprised, but as he talked on of his newly-stated convictions, Alexander agreed.[30] Arriving home in Washington, the talks continued.

> Through long days and nights father and son poured out their hearts concerning their religious experiences. Thomas Campbell had met Alexander with some trepidation of spirit, wondering how Alexander would receive the story of Thomas' unjust treatment by the American Presbytery and Synod and his decision to preach independently to audiences made up of people from all denominations. Strangely enough, Alexander, thousands of miles away, had been led by the Holy Spirit to an almost identical position. Finding themselves of one mind, they next began to discuss the *Declaration and Address.* Alexander gave his hearty approval to all the propositions. Captivated by its clear and decisive position, and thrilled by the opportunity to cast his lot with such a noble Christian enterprise, he shortly after informed his father that he had determined to consecrate his life to the dissemination and support of the principles and views set forth in the masterly document.[31]

The propositions of the *Declaration and Address* became the general guidelines for the work of reformation of the Campbells. Although Thomas Campbell authored the document, the preaching ability and later the writing of his son elevated Alexander to a natural leadership in propagating their ideas.

The *Declaration* was intended primarily for the Washington congregation. Placing emphasis upon the Scriptures as the only authoritative guidebook for Christians, it decried the evils of division and emphasized the desire to promote Christian unity. Nine resolutions followed which were intended to serve as a constitution for the Christian Association.

The main body, the *Address,* embodied the principles of Campbell for unity. It decried any idea of beginning a new denomination, hoping to accomplish unity of the existing denominations in brotherly love and fellowship. Thomas Campbell believed that every Christian had an obligation to work for unity and considered it the business of all, not just that of his own association.

> The cause that we advocate is not our own peculiar, nor the cause of any party, considered as such; it is a common cause, the cause of Christ and our brethren of all denominations. All that we presume, then, is to do what we humbly conceive to be *our* duty, in connexion with our brethren, to all of whom it equally belongs, as to us, to exert themselves for this blessed purpose. And as we have no just reason to doubt the concurrence of our brethren to accomplish an object so desirable in itself and fraught with such happy consequences, so neither can we look forward to that happy event, which will forever put an end to our hapless divisions, and restore to the Church its primitive unity, purity and prosperity, but in the pleasing prospect of their hearty and dutiful concurrence.[32]

The restoration of primitive Christianity became the slogan for the Campbell group. For them, bringing Christians together necessitated laying aside creeds and elevating the Bible as the only rule of authority. Thomas Campbell believed if this could be accomplished it would bring a restoration of the church of the New Testament. He sensed some, however, would think this absurd.

> Dearly beloved brethren, why should *we* deem it a thing incredible that the Church of Christ in this highly favoured country should resume that original unity, peace and purity, which belongs to its constitution, and contains its glory? Or, is there any thing that can be justly deemed necessary for this desirable purpose, but to conform to the model and adopt the practice of the primitive Church, expressly exhibited in the New Testament? Whatever alterations this might pro-

duce in any or all of the churches, should, we think, neither be deemed inadmissible nor ineligible. Surely such alterations would be every way for the better and not for the worse; unless we should suppose the divinely inspired rule to be faulty, or defective.[33]

Campbell did not ask other church bodies to join the Christian Association of Washington. He did propose that every church do away with creeds and remove anything from their worship services which lacked Biblical warrant. He called for reform and for an emerging leadership from the churches who were willing to adopt these principles. This seemed, to him, a simple proposition to accept, but it naturally met considerable opposition.

Division, Campbell believed, did not center in doctrinal matters of faith, but resulted primarily from opinions held in numerous areas.

It is, to us, a pleasing consideration that all the churches of Christ, which mutually acknowledge each other as such, are not only agreed in the great doctrines of faith and holiness, but are also materially agreed, as to the positive ordinances of Gospel institution; so that our differences at most, are about the things in which the kingdom of God does not consist, that is, about matters of private opinion, or human invention. What a pity that the kingdom of God should be divided about such things.[34]

He admitted that the Christian Association held some "educational prejudices and particular customs" which would require some struggle on their part to overcome. But, he added,

. . . this we do sincerely declare, that there is nothing we have hitherto received as a matter of faith or practice which is not expressly taught and enjoined in the word of God, either in express terms, or approved precedent, that we would not heartily relinquish, so that we might return to the original constitutional unity of the Christian Church, and, in this happy unity, enjoy full communion with all our brethren, in peace and charity.[35]

Matters of opinion, therefore, were private ground and

should not be enjoined upon one another. He encouraged others to show the same charitable attitude so that the "brethren of all denominations" might unite.[36]

Campbell argued that if unity was unachievable upon the basis of the Scriptures as the only book of authority, how could Christians ever unite? This was the only logical approach for him. All other methods were doomed to failure. Creeds, he stated, brought further division and offered no intention of drawing together those of different communions. The only alternative Campbell could see to his principles for unity was "voluntary compromise and good natured accommodation."[37]

Campbell made a strong plea for joining forces, reminding his readers that "there are no divisions in the grave; nor in that world which lies beyond it; there our divisions must come to an end."[38] "Unite with us in the common cause of simple, evangelical Christianity,"[39] he admonished his readers. "In this glorious cause we are ready to unite with you."[40]

Thirteen propositions followed the plea for unity which were "designed for opening up the way."[41] The propositions can be summarized as follows:

1. That the Church is essentially, intentionally, and constitutionally one, including all who profess faith in Christ and obedience to Him in all things.

2. That although the Church exists in local congregations, each should be charitable towards the others, receiving one another as brethren and walking by the same rule.

3. That nothing can be made conditions of fellowship and obligation except what is expressly taught in the Scriptures.

4. That although the two Testaments form the entire revelation of God and are inseparable, the New Testament is the perfect constitution for worship, discipline, and government of the New Testament Church.

5. That no human authority has power to impose new ordinances and commandments or add anything as a term of fellowship that is not as old as the New Testament.

6. That logical inferences and deductions from Scripture based on human wisdom cannot be made binding upon the consciences of other Christians any further than they understand them.

7. That inferential truths resulting from human logic ought not be made conditions of fellowship since not all Christians attain the same degree of knowledge.

8. That Church membership is conditioned upon profession of faith in Christ and obedience to Him, and not upon attaining a particular degree of knowledge of Scripture.

9. That all who make this profession are children of the same Father and should treat one another as brothers.

10. That division among the children of God is anti-Christian, anti-Scriptural, anti-natural, and produces confusion.

11. That all division can be traced to either a partial neglect of the Scriptures or making human innovations conditions of fellowship.

12. That purity of the Church is contingent upon a pure membership and a qualified ministry that follow the example of the primitive church.

13. That any human expedients necessary to this endeavor must make no pretense to sacred origin so that future changes in them will not produce contention or division.[42]

While Campbell stated his opposition to creeds he did not condemn them unconditionally. His opposition to creeds stood

> . . . only in *so far* as they oppose the unity of the Church by containing sentiments not expressly revealed in the Word of God, or, by the way of using them, become the instruments of a human or implicit faith, or oppress the weak of God's heritage. When they are liable to none of these objections, we have nothing against them. It is the *abuse* and not the *lawful use* of such compilations that we oppose.[43]

He made no claim to perfection for his series of propositions and hastened to add that if he had missed the way he desired that others would set him on the right course. But, he added, if he had stated "obvious and undeniable truths which, if adopted and acted upon, would infallibly lead to the desired unity," then he urged acceptance. "Union in Truth" was his motto.[44] Such were the plans for unity Thomas Cambell outlined.

Publication of the pamphlet brought varied response from religious leaders. Several ministerial friends of Thomas Campbell read the publication and personally received the principles with a certain degree of kindness, but would not take any active part in publicly advocating them without some assurance of success.[45] Others, fearful of the propositions, became alarmed and maintained a watchful eye on the progress of the Christian Association.[46] For the most part, however, the document had little effect on the religious climate at that time.[47] The spread of the reformation of the Campbell's came as Alexander assumed the leadership of the movement.

Shortly after Alexander Campbell arrived in Washington he formed an acquaintance with Lawyer Mountain of Pittsburgh. Alexander impressed Mr. Mountain with his character and abilities and he offered Campbell a sizeable sum of money and other inducements to take charge of an academy. He declined the offer, stating that he intended to do everything within his power to promote the principles of the *Declaration and Address* and that both tasks would be too much for him.[48] When he informed his father of this decision the elder Campbell requested that he take up a study of the Bible for six months without any interference.[49]

ALEXANDER CAMPBELL AND THE STRUGGLE FOR IDENTITY

Alexander Campbell delivered his first public address in 1810. His father had, for some time, expressed his desire for Alexander to participate in the public gatherings. Like most first attempts, it was not notable or outstanding but it pleased his father. The audience quickly concluded that he held the upper hand over his father in speaking ability.[50] Starting from that first experience on July 15, 1810, he preached 106 sermons during his first full year, speaking at various places in Western Pennsylvania, Virginia, and Eastern Ohio. While he gained some popularity in advocating his father's principles of union he believed the lack of affiliation with a church group hindered the work.

Thomas Campbell had attempted to correct this situation with an application on October 2, 1810, to the Synod of Pittsburgh, which was meeting in Washington, for affiliation with the Presbyterian Church. The charter presented for the Christian Association was the *Declaration and Address.* The Synod refused this request, stating that (1) Campbell believed the Confession of Faith of the Presbyterians contained some things not found in Scripture; (2) he believed infant baptism was not authorized by Scripture, yet administered it while holding these views; (3) he permitted his son to preach without regular authority; and (4) he opposed creeds as injurious to religion.[51] Obviously this was not an attempt by the Campbells to unite on Presbyterian principles, but to gain a larger identity for their work.[52] The decision of the Synod should not be surprising; too many differences existed.

Organization into an independent church came to the Christian Association on May 4, 1811, for "the enjoyment of those privileges and the performances of those duties which belong to church relations."[53] The members appointed Thomas Campbell as elder, licensed Alexander to preach, and selected four deacons; John Dawson, John Foster, George Sharp and William Gilcrist.[54] Their building also served as a community building and desiring a building entirely their own, they erected a new frame structure on propety donated by Gilcrist. They named it Brush Run and occupied it for the first time on June 16, 1811.[55]

They soon began to question having organized into an independent church, wondering if they were acting correctly. While asking for unity and seeking for an end to division, they had formed their own little body; exactly what Thomas

Campbell did not want at the beginning. They wanted fellowship with a larger body, but there seemed to be no group to whom they could turn since the Presbyterians had refused them. As time passed the Campbells came to the conclusion in 1812 that immersion was the correct form of baptism and both father and son were immersed.[56] Alexander now began to lean toward the Baptists and preached often in their congregations, and, in 1812, attended the Redstone Association meeting at Uniontown, Pennsylvania.[57] He expressed his disappointment with the preaching at this meeting and decided he would not attend any more. He learned, however, that the Baptist people also regarded the preaching inferior to what they were accustomed to receiving and reconsidered. Their invitation to Campbell to join their association received the approval of the Brush Run congregation and they applied for membership.[58] They resolved, for the benefit of the Redstone Association, to write down their beliefs.

> We did so in some eight or ten pages of large dimensions, exhibiting our remonstrance against all human creeds as bonds of communion or union amongst Christian Churches, and expressing a willingness, upon certain conditions, to co-operate or unite with that Association, provided always that we should be allowed to teach and preach whatever we learned from the Holy Scriptures, regardless of any creed or formula in Christendom.[59]

A small group opposed the reception of Brush Run into the Association and continued to offer some resistance,[60] but a good relationship lasted for the next three years. Shortly after this union Thomas Campbell thought he had accomplished all he could in that area and decided to sell his property and move to Guernsey County, Ohio. He planned to purchase a farm and also start a seminary in Cambridge and two of his sons-in-law, Joseph Bryant and Andrew Chapman, agreed to go with him to assist.[62]

Greater resistance came toward Campbell as a result of events that led up to and included the meeting of the Redstone Association at Cross Creek church near Wellsburg, Virginia, in 1816. Campbell had moved from the Brush Run area to a farm near Wellsburg in 1814.[63] The next year he proposed that a church building be built in Wellsburg and he volunteered to make a tour through the east to raise the funds. He succeeded in raising $1,000.00 and the building was built in 1816. This created a problem with John Pritchard, minister at Cross Creek Baptist church, because his congregation was only three miles from Wellsburg. He viewed this as an attempt to weaken his influence and diminish his congregration. As the host minister for the Redstone Association meeting in August, 1816, he attempted to use his influence and position to keep Campbell from preaching, claiming that since Campbell was so close the people could hear him anytime and preachers who had traveled the farthest distance should be heard. His efforts were defeated since so many wanted to hear Campbell, who chose his text from Romans 8:3 and preached his "Sermon on the Law,"[64] which since has recognition as one of his finest sermons. Pritchard spoke to others after this sermon attempting to get the Association to censure Campbell, but other ministers who were consulted thought any action of that nature would bring more adverse feelings toward them than toward Campbell. Consequently they decided to inform the churches of his antinomianism and hope to avert some of his influence.[65] Campbell answered these charges by printing his sermon in pamphlet form and circulating it. When the Redstone Association met the next year at Peter's Creek his opponents unsuccessfully attempted to have the sermon condemned, but the matter was dismissed on the basis that the Association had no jurisdiction in the matter.[66] By the time that Campbell preached his "Sermon on the Law" his biographer estimates that his group numbered about 150 adherents scattered among the Baptists over a three-state area.[67]

Alexander Campbell started Buffaloe Seminary in January, 1818.[68] Thomas Campbell had moved to Kentucky but Alexander asked him to return to minister to the Brush Run Church and help with the seminary.[69] The early days of the college were disappointing to the younger Campbell because most of the students pursued a classical education with little interest in the ministry.

In looking for events that had later impact on the movement Alexander Campbell's debate with John Walker, minister of the Secession Church at Mount Pleasant, Ohio, stands as a key event. Campbell entered the debate at the urging of John Birch, a Baptist preacher near there. The debate was held on June 19-20, 1820, on the subject of baptism.[70] The debate was published and helped spread the influence of Campbell.

Probably the reading of the printed copies of the debate had more of a lasting influence on the Campbell movement than the actual debate, especially by one reader, Adamson Bentley. Bentley was a Baptist minister at Warren, Ohio, on the Western Reserve. He influenced the ministers of the area to have annual meetings on the Reserve that ultimately developed into the Mahoning Baptist Association. After reading the debate he visited Campbell in 1821 and influenced him to attend the meetings of the Mahoning Association.[71]

The ministers in the Redstone Association who disagreed with Campbell's views had gained the necessary support by August, 1823, to expel him from the Association. When Campbell learned of this he lacked the time to prepare an adequate defense, having scheduled another debate on baptism, this one at Augusta, Kentucky, with W.A. McCalla, a Presbyterian minister.[72] Campbell feared that a censure or expulsion would harm his position for the debate. Although he lived near Wellsburg he had retained membership at Brush Run, and his affiliation with Redstone was through that congregation. In order to avoid the problem, Campbell and several other members asked for letters of dismissal from Brush Run to start a new church in Wellsburg. Since the new congregation had no affiliation with Redstone Association no action could be taken against Campbell due to lack of jurisdiction.[73] Campbell later united with the Mahoning Baptist Association, a union which had far reaching effects throughout Ohio.

Why did the union with the Redstone Association fail? Richardson blames the jealousy of the other ministers toward Campbell and the differences of ideas.[74] W.T. Moore concluded that the only similarity in beliefs were church organization and baptism, while numerous differences existed: (1) the work of the Holy Spirit in conversion, (2) the differences between the Old and New Testaments, (3) ordination and authority of the ministry, (4) method of administration and frequency of the Lord's Supper, (5) the means of receiving remission of sins, (6) the Trinity, and (7) Christian experience connected with conversion.[75] While the possibilities of this union working seemed insurmountable without some change in beliefs by the ministers in Redstone Association, obviously Campbell must have entertained thoughts of that occurring. But Alexander Campbell's first experience at union had failed.

EXTENDING THE INFLUENCE

Campbell turned to writing in 1823 as a means of propagating his views, starting a monthly publication called *The Christian Baptist*. It served its purpose well, especially in the state of Kentucky, where some of its most avid readers became converts to Campbell's views and leaders of the movement.[76] Since so many of these were from the Baptist churches they became known as the Reformed Baptists or simply Reformers.

Alexander Campbell, according to his biographer, developed his own principles for Christian unity and engaged in advocating those of his father only because they closely paralleled his. Richardson gives the greatest credit for molding young Campbell's ideas to Greville Ewing,[77] the minister of the Congregational Church in Glasgow which Campbell attended on Sunday nights while in Glasgow. Through listening to him preach and by personal interviews Campbell learned the principles of independence and congregational government.[78]

Creeds and confessions also presented questions for Campbell while he was still in Scotland. Although his faith in them was "considerably shaken" while in Scotland, he did not oppose them until he witnessed the numerous divisions created by them in the United States. He concluded that creeds were "bones of controversy, the seeds of discord, the cause as well as the effect of division."[79] In 1823 he wrote:

> But as Christians have never yet all possessed the same prejudices, degrees of information, passions, interests, modes of thinking and reasoning, and the same strength of understanding, an attempt to associate them under the banner of a human creed composed of human inferences, and requiring unanimity in the adoption of it, is every way as irrational as to make a uniformity of features, of color, of height and weight, a bond of union.[80]

While his father opposed creeds only as far as they were misused, Alexander detested them. He believed the absolute destruction of creeds would be essential before Christian unity could be achieved.[81]

Human opinions as matters of faith could occupy no room in Christianity if unity were achieved, according to Campbell. This meant that essential matters of faith must be identified so that some standard could be supported. Campbell narrowed this to the area of salvation, contending that this must be based upon the Bible. The only basis, he believed, that could be imposed upon anyone was belief in a single fact and submission to a single institution. This one fact was the deity of Jesus — that He was the Son of God. Each person who came to this belief must submit to one institution; baptism in water. Belief of this one fact and demonstration of that belief by submission to the institution of baptism made one a child of God.[82] Campbell believed that on this foundation all human opinion could be excluded and the church could have unity.

Confronted by the fact that in Campbell's theology, baptism meant immersion, this issue received strong opposition and attacks from those outside Baptist bodies. One opponent later wrote,

> It is true, he cares not whether we are Arians, Socinians, or Universalists; in this he is very liberal in his commands; but then, we must adopt his notions of the efficacy of baptism and receive it according to his *ipse dixit,* or he pronounces us "unpardoned, and lost to all christian life and enjoyment." Very moderate indeed![83]

He then penned a short piece of satirical poetry illustrative of his general concept of Campbell's views.

> I little care what men believe,
> Provided they my faith receive,
> And come to me, with me unite,
> And think my views and plans are right;
> And swear allegiance to the water—
> As for the rest, 'tis little matter.[84]

Campbell, however, continued to expand his influence through debating, preaching, and writing. The number of followers grew as more became familiar with him and his ideas. If his thinking in regard to Christian unity could be reduced to a single statement it would be:

> *Let* THE BIBLE *be substituted for all human creeds;* FACTS, *for definitions;* THINGS, *for words;* FAITH, *for speculation;* UNITY OF FAITH, *for unity of opinion;* THE POSITIVE COMMANDS of God, *for* human legislation and tradition; PIETY, *for ceremony;* MORALITY, *for partizan zeal;* THE PRACTICE OF RELIGION, *for the profession of it,* — and the work is done.[85]

By 1826 the Campbells had laid the foundation for their work of reformation, but could only look back at the accomplishments with a small degree of satisfaction. But the foundations had been well placed, and an emerging future of success was ready to unfold.

CHAPTER SUMMARY

Thomas Campbell came to America with some well-formed views on independent church government and Christian unity and soon found himself in a position to freely espouse them. Censured by the Presbytery of Chartiers, Campbell was left with no appointments for preaching. Using private homes and shaded groves for his pulpit, he gathered a group together and formed The Christian Association of Washington. Soon after this formation he penned the *Declaration and Address* which was printed and widely distributed with hopes of promoting Christian unity. While Thomas Campbell was completing this document his family, including his son Alexander, arrived in America. Within a short time Alexander's abilities placed him at the leadership of the movement.

Christian unity was the central theme of the *Declaration and Address* and was considered a "darling theme" by Alexander Campbell. As they struggled for identity they attempted to find affiliation with the Synod of Pittsburgh, offering the

Declaration and Address as their charter. Refused admission by the Synod, they turned to the Baptists who permitted Alexander to preach in several of their churches. They organized the Brush Run Church in 1811 and were granted membership into the Redstone Baptist Association. All went well until Alexander preached his "Sermon on the Law" at the association meeting in 1816, creating opposition to his position. Leaving the Redstone Association in 1823, he later united with the Mahoning Baptist Association in Ohio which proved to be an excellent decision. Through debates, preaching, and the pages of *The Christian Baptist* Alexander Campbell extended his influence into several states, particularly in Ohio, Kentucky, Indiana, and Virginia. He developed the concept of the restoration of the ancient order of things, calling for a return to the Scriptures alone for practice as well as authority and doctrine.

1. For a brief account of the different divisions in the Presbyterian Church in Scotland which placed Thomas Campbell into the Anti-Burgher Seceder faction of that body in Ireland, see James DeForest Murch, *Christians Only* (Cincinnati: Standard Publishing Company, 1962), pp. 37-38.

2. Alexander Campbell, *Memoirs of Elder Thomas Campbell* (Cincinnati: H.S. Bosworth, 1861), p. 9.

3. Robert Richardson, *Memoirs of Alexander Campbell*, Volume I (Nashville: Gospel Advocate Co., 1956), p. 58.

4. Campbell, *Memoirs*, p. 116.

5. *Ibid.*

6. W.T. Moore, *A Comprehensive History of the Disciples of Christ* (New York: Fleming H. Revell Co., 1909), p. 99.

7. Murch, p. 39.

8. *Ibid.*

9. *Ibid.*

10. Moore, p. 99.

11. Murch, p. 39

12. Moore, p. 103.

13. *Ibid.*

14. Murch, p. 39.

15. Campbell, *Memoirs*, p. 40.

16. Murch, p. 40.

17. *Ibid.*

18. Richardson, p. 235.

19. *Ibid,* p. 238.
20. *Ibid.*
21. *Ibid.*
22. *Ibid.*
23. *Ibid,* p.239.
24. *Ibid,* p. 240.
25. *Ibid,* p. 241.
26. *Ibid.*
27. *Ibid,* pp. 241-242.
28. Murch, p. 42.
29. Richardson, pp. 194-220.
30. *Ibid,* pp. 220-221.
31. Murch, p. 57.
32. Thomas Campbell, *Declaration and Address* (Birmingham: The Berean Press, 1941), p. 9.
33. *Ibid,* pp. 9-10.
34. *Ibid,* p. 10.
35. *Ibid.*
36. *Ibid.*
37. *Ibid,* p. 11.
38. *Ibid,* p. 12.
39. *Ibid.*
40. *Ibid.*
41. *Ibid,* p. 14.
42. Frederick D. Kershner has summarized these propositions and they are cited in different works. For example, see Murch, p. 47. Some of the original thought is lost in his summary that seems important to an understanding of Thomas Campbell at that point of time in his life. Every summary, naturally, has the problem of not conveying all the thoughts, but these are presented with the intention of including as much of the original thoughts as possible in this type of a summation.
43. Thomas Campbell, p. 23.
44. *Ibid,* pp. 17-18.
45. Richardson, p. 311.
46. *Ibid.*
47. Murch, p. 50.
48. Richardson, pp. 274-275.
49. *Ibid,* p. 275.
50. *Ibid,* pp. 316-317.
51. *Ibid,* p. 328.
52. *Ibid,* p. 329.
53. Moore, p. 131.
54. Richardson, p. 367.
55. *Ibid,* p. 371. At the present only a small marker standing in a brushy corner of a wooded area marks the place where this building once stood.
56. *Ibid,* pp. 393-405.
57. Alexander Campbell, "Address to the Public," *The Christian Baptist,* Volume II (September, 1824), p. 37.
58. Richardson, p. 440.
59. *Ibid,* pp. 440-441.
60. *Ibid,* p. 441.

61. *Ibid*, pp. 458-459.

62. *Ibid*, p. 459.

63. *Ibid*, pp. 460-461. Several members of Brush Run, including Campbell, had planned to move west to Zanesville, Ohio. John Brown, Campbell's father-in-law, did not want to see part of his family so far away and gave his farm to Campbell to move to and work. Brown moved to Wellsburg (Charlestown) and opened a grocery business and attended the Cross Creek church.

64. Discovery of some of Alexander Campbell's papers in Australia revealed this was not a new topic for him since he had preached a sermon by the same topic at Brush Run on October 23, 1812. See Alger M. Fitch, Jr., "Recent Developments in the Study of Alexander Campbell," *Christian Standard*, (March 13, 1965), p. 164.

65. Richardson, pp. 464-472.

66. *Ibid*, p. 479.

67. *Ibid*, p. 488.

68. *Ibid*, pp. 491-492.

69. *Ibid*, pp. 496-497.

70. Robert Richardson, *Memoirs of Alexander Campbell*, Volume II, (Nashville: Gospel Advocate Company, 1956), pp. 14-18.

71. *Ibid*, p. 45.

72. Murch, p. 76.

73. Richardson, Volume II, pp. 68-70.

74. *Ibid*, pp. 68-69.

75. Moore, pp. 158-161.

76. John Rogers recorded in his unpublished journal (p. 166) that the paper was so well received in Kentucky that soon the ones who had opposed Barton W. Stone and his followers now turned their attention toward Campbell.

77. Richardson, Volume I, p. 148.

78. *Ibid*, p. 187.

79. Alexander Campbell, "A Restoration of the Ancient Order of Things," (Number 3), *The Christian Baptist*, Volume II, (April, 1825), p. 174.

80. Alexander Campbell, "A Restoration of the Ancient Order of Things," (Number 2), *The Christian Baptist*, Volume II, (March, 1825), p. 155.

81. Alexander Campbell, "Christian Union," *The Christian Baptist*, Volume II, (July, 1825), p. 234.

82. Alexander Campbell, "The Foundation of Hope and of Christian Union," *The Christian Baptist*, Volume I, (April, 1824), pp. 176-178.

83. William Phillips, *Campbellism Exposed; or, Strictures on the Peculiar Tenets of Alexander Campbell*, (Cincinnati: Poe and Hitchcock, 1861), pp. 202-203.

84. *Ibid*, p. 203.

85. Alexander Campbell, *Schism, Its Bane and Antidote; or, The True Foundation of Christian Union* (London: Simpkin and Co., R. Groombridge; and T. Kirk, 1840), p. 9.

3

GROWTH, SIMILARITIES, AND DIFFERENCES

INTRODUCTION

Following Alexander Campbell's entrance into Kentucky in 1823 to debate, numerous people from the Baptist segment subscribed to his periodical, *The Christian Baptist,* who soon subscribed also to his principles, creating turmoil among the Baptists in Kentucky. Those who accepted Campbell's ideas were called Reformers and were bitterly opposed by the main-line Baptists. This opposition drew the Reformers toward the Christians since both advocated some of the same concepts. Differences also existed in some areas, but other factors made the differences secondary, producing a climate for union between the two groups.

THE RISE OF THE REFORMED BAPTISTS IN KENTUCKY

The reformation of the Campbells had made little impact

in Kentucky by the time the first copy of *The Christian Messenger,* edited by Barton W. Stone, came from the press in 1826. Campbell's appearance in Kentucky in 1823 for the debate on baptism with McCalla gained him some credibility among the Baptists of that state. It also brought several subscriptions to his periodical, *The Christian Baptist.* Campbell apparently withheld the introduction of his periodical in Kentucky until this debate, believing that it would be more readily accepted.[1] A prospectus for *The Christian Baptist* was given to John Smith of Mount Sterling who immediately subscribed to the paper and encouraged others to do the same.[2] Smith, a Baptist preacher, became one of the important leaders of the Reformers in Kentucky.

Campbell's concern centered more in bringing reformation to existing churches instead of beginning new ones. Therefore, his early work did not possess a strong evangelistic fervor. Several congregations had by 1827 left their original positions and accepted reformation principles, the earliest known of these occurring at Hiram, Ohio, on August 21, 1824.[3]

In the fall of 1824 Alexander Campbell made another journey to Kentucky to become better acquainted with the religious situation and gain personal acquaintances with some of the more noted leaders among the Baptists. During this three-months' journey, he met John Smith, Jacob Creath, Sr., Jacob Creath, Jr., Dr. Silas M. Noel, James Challen, and P.S. Fall.[4] He considered the Kentucky Baptists a different type than those of his home area and concluded their religious concepts were not far from his, making the state a fertile field for propogating his views.

P.S. Fall of Louisville is credited with being the "first resident Baptist minister in Kentucky to take his stand openly in favor of the principles of the Reformation."[5] He had read, as early as 1823, the "Sermon on the Law" and had publicly expounded these principles at Frankfort.[6] Others followed, leading to a great revival in the Baptist churches in Kentucky in 1828, making a significant impact on the reformation. John Rogers reported that "hundreds and thousands were immersed among them, in the north of Kentucky, principally by those preachers who were very much under the influence of A. Campbell."[7] Many Baptist leaders viewed this rapid growth as a threat to the power structure of the numerous Baptist Associations in Kentucky. The old-line preachers saw no alternative to the situation except direct encounter.

When the messengers gave reports at the North District Association in 1828, the Reformer-dominated churches reported large numbers of additions. John Smith's three congregations alone reported 392 baptisms. Nearly 900 baptisms, most of them converts of Smith, were reported by twenty-four churches. He had also started five new churches based on reformation ideas which became members of the association.[8]

The Lulbegrud Church had filed charges in 1827 against one of the preachers, apparently not naming him in the charge, which the North District Association had to hear. These charges were:

> 1. That, while it is the custom of the Baptists to use as the word of God King James translation, he had on two or three occasions in public, and often privately in his family devotions, read from Alexander Campbell's translation.
> 2. That, while it is the custom in the ceremony of baptism to pronounce, "I baptize you," he on the contrary is in the habit of saying, "I immerse you."
> 3. That, in administering the Lord's Supper, while it is the custom to break the loaf into bits, small enough to be readily taken into the mouth, yet he leaves the bread in pieces, teaching that each communicant should break it for himself.[9]

Smith, listening to the charges, immediately realizing that he was the preacher in question, arose and said, "I plead guilty to them all."[10] When the delegates from the churches arrived the Reformers were clearly in the majority and the charges were never officially made. But the seeds of division were evident and in 1830 ten churches withdrew and formed a new association, while the Reformers continued another year in the old one, finally disbanding in 1832.[11]

The Bracken Association, with a membership in 1828 of 2,200, also faced a problem with the Reformers, a dispute that lasted over the next two years. The Licking Association had made a request to Bracken to enter into mutual correspondence but, being decidedly Calvinistic, asked Bracken for a pledge to the Philadelphia Confession of Faith. When the issue came to the point of a resolution, the Reformers succeeded in passing a resolution recommending no creed but the New Testament. By 1830 membership had fallen to 900, some of the Calvinistic Baptists having joined the Licking Association, others remaining aloof from any body, but a large majority of this defection were Reformers.[12]

The name of John Smith appears in the records of the Boone's Creek Association in 1828 as it also experienced problems. During the spring and summer of 1828, 870 people had been immersed in the bounds of the association, many through the efforts of John Smith. This group, composed of thirteen churches, entertained a resolution at their meeting in September, 1828, recommending the abolition of the present constitution and authoritative association, replacing it with a general meeting for worship and communication regarding the state of the churches. Seven congregations voted to retain the constitution and six favored its repeal. The six churches were dropped from the association in 1830.[13]

Tate's Creek Association, totaling twenty-six churches in its body, also was Reformer-dominated by 1829. The next year a minority of those churches withdrew, called a special meeting, and re-organized the association. They listed what they considered errors of the Reformers, determining to have no correspondence with the churches that tolerated "Camp-

ɔellism." Ten of the twenty-six churches sent delegates, in-
dicative that the majority of the congregations were under
Reformer influence.[14] Membership in the association churches dropped from 2,661 to 932, indicating that nearly two-
thirds of the association membership had accepted Reformer
principles.[15]

Two other associations, South Concord and Long Run,
also lost members to the Reformers; South Concord losing
about one-fourth of its membership and Long Run losing five
churches.[16] The Concord Association, meeting in session at
Hopwell in Henry County on October 27, 1830, took a firm
stand against the Reformers' infiltration of their churches and
the doctrines of the Reformers.

> We believe the churches should not invite them to preach in their
> meeting houses. That we should not invite them into our houses to
> preach, nor in any way bid them God speed, nor their heretical doc-
> trine. We advise you brethren to be particularly on your guard. When
> they are talking about the Spirit, we believe they only mean the Writ-
> ten Word, and when they speak of regeneration, they only mean im-
> mersion in water.[17]

The Russell's Creek Association passed a similar resolution at
its meeting at Pitman's Creek Church on September 18,
1830.[18] Elkhorn Association lost 1,100 members to the
Reformers in 1830 alone, having previously lost thirty-five
churches by dismissal and expulsion during the 1820's.[19]
Bethel and Green River Associations were among the last to
act against the Reformers, in 1831.[20]

The Reformers emerged in Kentucky, principally, from
Baptist roots. Able preachers, who became bulwarks for the
Reformers, notably John Smith, P.S. Fall, Jacob Creath, Sr.,
and Jacob Creath, Jr., were excluded from associations during
this turbulent situation. Some new congregations were
started by men who examined the teachings of Campbell and
then withdrew from Baptists. The most notable of these was

John T. Johnson, who started a congregation at Great Crossings.[21]

The Reformers had so decimated some of the associations in Kentucky that one person stated that if the Lord had not been on the side of the Baptists, the "Campbellites" would have completely overrun them in Kentucky.[22] The loss to the Baptist Church is more realistically stated by another historian.

> The available statistics of the Baptists in Kentucky in 1829 give thrity-four associations, six hundred fourteen churches, and 45,442 members; but the report in 1830 showed a loss of forty churches and 5,485 members largely as a result of the division. In 1832, an additional decrease of 4,095 was reported, which made a total loss of 9,580 members in three years. The total membership in 1832 was 35,862. . . .[23]

Loss to the Baptist Church alone does not give an accurate estimate of the size of the Reformers in Kentucky by 1832. Evangelistic efforts brought great numbers of accessions into the churches during the time span of 1828-1832, especially in the Reformer-dominated churches, and it obviously follows that many of these numerous converts were never included in any of the Baptist association figures.

A major thrust of the Reformers' ideals focused on the theme of Christian unity, yet it soon became apparent that they would not remain united with the Baptists. Masters cites two events that contributed to the demise of relationship between the two groups, each group making its single contribution in 1830.[24] The first wedge came from the pen of Alexander Campbell with the publication of his "Extra on Remission of Sins."

> The document contained sixty pages, and was distributed so as to reach all the associations, which were to meet in late summer and early autumn. After the publication of the "Extra" there was no longer any doubt as to Mr. Campbell's position on the design of baptism, be-

ing essential to the salvation of the soul. This document hastened the day when Mr. Campbell's followers would be separated from the Baptists. Dr. B.H. Carroll, of Texas, said, "When he brought out that 'Extra' the 'fur began to fly.' "[25]

The Baptists made their contribution to the separation at a meeting of the Franklin Association, in special session, at Frankfort in July. Nineteen churches of the association and representatives from five other associations attended. Cited as "probably the most important called session of any association ever held in Kentucky." Masters wrote,

> The principal object of it was to define Campbellism, and to warn the churches against its devastating influence. This was done in a circular letter printed in the minutes and sent to all the churches in the Association. This letter was written by "the learned, profound and eminently godly Silas M. Noel," which set forth in a clear positive statement the teachings of Alexander Campbell, taken from his own writings. This circular letter was scattered among the churches in all the associations before their meetings, later that year. The letter contained an introduction and thirty-nine Articles extracted from Mr. Campbell's two periodicals — *The Christian Baptist* and *The Millennial Harbinger*.[26]

Campbell responded to the letter in the September issue of *The Millennial Harbinger* by attacking the spirit of the leaders in the associations, charging that their only allies were "church councils, creeds and majorities."[27] He did not print the letter.

SIMILARITIES OF REFORMERS AND CHRISTIANS

While the Baptists and Reformers were moving in separate directions, the Christians of Stone's group made notable growth, possibly numbering as many as 10,000 members by 1831.[28] The problems which the Reformers experienced with the Baptists drew them toward the Christians, largely because groups of both bodies quite analogous in doctrine existed in the same communities but met in separate assemblies. Why, questioned some, did not the two groups unite?

The leaders of both groups advocated Christian unity based solely upon the Bible, with all human speculations and opinions cast aside in regard to Christian fellowship. John Rogers stated that Stone first advocated the union of Christians upon the Bible alone, but "It was reserved for A. Campbell . . . to prepound to the Christian world the true basis for Christian Union — the Union of all the true followers of Christ."[29]

Reproach from the Christian community toward both bodies gave them another common denominator. Stone had earlier expressed some opinions, what he termed "speculations," on the doctrines of the Godhead and atonement, bringing constant harassment upon the Christians as Arians and Socinians. The Reformers of the North District had united with the Calvinists in an association resolution in 1828 against communion with the Chrstians.[30] The Reformers soon found that same spirit of reproach turned upon them, largely because of their doctrinal position regarding baptism.

> A common reproach daily weakened their prejudices against each other, and quickened the growth of sympathy between them, and they began at last to feel the differences of opinion ought not to keep apart those who were one in faith and purpose, and who had, in fact, with equal firmness, renounced opinion as a bond of union among the children of God.[31]

The third similarity that contributed to their willingness to consider union was independence and congregational government. Stone moved to this position during his formative years in Kentucky and his break with the Presbyterians, while Campbell had learned it from Ewing while still in Scotland. Following Campbell's thinking, the Reformers in Kentucky urged an end to authoritative associations and replacement with annual meetings for fellowship, creating the opportunity for congregational interaction between the two bodies.

DIFFERENCES

They did not, however, agree on every issue, and the differences required gentle treatment.[32] Campbell and Stone differed on the Godhead, atonement, and the nature of Christ, but these issues presented no serious problem because they did not flow down to the rank and file. They differed on the name, Stone preferring "Christian" and Campbell expressing a preference for "Disciple."

John Rogers, a Christian minister, pointed to three major difficulties which many of the Christians had with Campbell and the Reformers. These comprised the largest hurdle for the Christians in effecting the union.

> 1. They feared he was not sound on the subject of spiritual influence. That he did not believe in heart-religion. That religion with him was more intellectual than spiritual.
> 2. They had difficulties on the question of baptism for remission of sins — they thought in believing in baptism for remission, they denied their own Christian experience and doomed all the pious pedo-baptists to ruin.
> 3. They could not see the fitness, and propriety of taking the Lord's Supper every Lord's day. They argued it would become common, and lose its sacredness and efficacy.[33]

Campbell maintained that the Holy Spirit operated on the hearts of sinners only through preaching or reading of the Scriptures. The Christians, having their roots in the camp meetings, would not permit such limitations upon the sphere of operation of the Holy Ghost.

The difficulties over baptism for the remission of sins were never totally resolved for all of the Christians. Although a large number of them came to that position, including John

Rogers, many in Ohio and Indiana rejected the concept and ultimately opposed union. The use of the mourners's bench among the Christian Churches made the doctrine of remission of sins through baptism offensive. Still, a minor argument arose over who first preached the doctrine of remission of sins by baptism. Samuel Rogers, a brother of John, gave the credit to Stone, citing a situation at Millersburg, Ky., in 1821, as evidence. Several mourners, according to his account, found no release from their agonies as they prayed around the bench to a very late hour. Stone labored with them until finally, in a bewildered state himself because of the apparent failure of the mourners to find relief, he arose and addressed the audience.

> Brethren, something must be wrong; we have been laboring with these mourners earnestly, and they are deeply penitent; why have they not found relief? We all know that God is willing to pardon them, and certainly they are anxious to receive it. The cause must be that we do not preach as the Apostles did. On the day of Pentecost, those who "were pierced to the heart" were promptly told what to do for the remission of sins. And "they gladly received the word, and were baptized; and the same day about three thousand were added unto them." He then quoted the commission: "He that believeth and is baptized shall be saved."[34]

This immediately "dampened" the meeting, according to Rogers, but Stone attempted to preach baptism for the remission of sins elsewhere, finally giving it up because "the people were by no means prepared for this doctrine."[35] The evidence seems quite conclusive that, although Stone may have preached it first, most of the preachers of the Christian Church learned the doctrine from Campbell, largely by reading the debate with McCalla[36] and other of Campbell's writings. Even John Rogers, probably the most notable of the Christian ministers, with the exception of Stone, stated that Campbell "developed to us not only the true design of baptism, but also the true basis of Christian union."[37] This indicates the doctrine of baptism for the remission of sins came primarily through Campbell.

Regardless of one's position regarding the purpose of baptism, should baptism stand as a condition of fellowship? Stone and Campbell apparently differed strongly on this. Stone wrote, "... I am not yet prepared to reject from fellowship all, not immersed for the remission of sins. If I understand him (Campbell), he does."[38] Claiming that he was as fully convinced on the issue of immersion for the remission of sins as Campbell, Stone wrote,

> ... yet I remember the people of God have been long in the wilderness, and have been misled to the neglect of this ordinance; as the Israelites of old neglected a divine command, (circumcision) when in the wilderness between Egypt and Canaan. I have no doubt that speaking and urging the truth in love, with christian forbearance, will ultimately effect what a contrary course will fail to do.[39]

While Stone's attitude toward the unimmersed remained cordial, he held some reservations regarding their position, admitting that he would not consider them "*christians* in the full sense of the term."[40]

The issue of the Lord's supper presented some theological differences, but in practice the Christians believed the rites of baptism and the Lord's supper could only be administered by ordained ministers. Since the Christians suffered from a shortage of ordained ministers, weekly communion as advocated by Campbell presented a problem. While Stone agreed with Campbell that, "whenever the church shall be restored to her former glory, she will again receive the Lord's supper on every first day of the week,"[41] several of the Christian ministers were not in agreement with their leader on this issue. Additionally, ordination into the ministry included women for the Christians, while the Reformers rejected this.[42]

Foot washing, while not practiced among the Reformers, did have some advocates among the Christians, ascribed to the home as a family matter but not to the church. He drew his conclusions from the observance of the Passover in family units, unless the family was small, which in such cases permitted families to share together. When Jesus partook of the Passover and washed the disciples' feet, Stone asserted, it was a family affair; the family of Jesus. Lodging strangers, argued Stone, would be just as much a church ordinance as washing feet.[43] Again, on this issue, many of the Christians did not concur with Stone and practiced foot-washing as a church ordinance, especially in Ohio and Indiana.[44]

The similarities of the Christians and Reformers, at least in Kentucky, outweighed the differences. More is required, however, to bring two religious bodies of this nature together than just some similarities of doctrine and practice. The similarities, impersonal in nature, certainly played their role in effecting the union in Kentucky, but the most significant factors were the personal ones; the people who acted from unselfish motives.

CHAPTER SUMMARY

Campbell viewed his work more in perspective of reformation rather than evangelism with his greatest impact coming among the Baptist churches, particularly in Kentucky. A rupture came in this arrangement when Campbell published his "Extra on Remission of Sins" in which he expressed his position on baptism, a view contrary to Baptist doctrine. As the Reformers drew away from the Baptists they recognized an affinity with the Christians in their pleas for unity, congregational government, and the reproach of others in the Christian community toward both groups. Differences prevailed over the Godhead, the atonement, the nature of Christ, the work of the Holy Spirit in conversion, baptism for the remission of sins, the Lord's supper, and foot washing.

Some of these differences were more important to the leaders, Campbell and Stone, than to the rank and file and did not stand as significant hindrances to union in Kentucky.

---

1. Richardson, *Memoirs,* Volume II, p. 87.

2. John Augustus Williams, *Life of Elder John Smith* (Nashville: Gospel Advocate Company, 1956), p. 117.

3. Alanson Wilcox, *A History of the Disciples of Christ in Ohio* (Cincinnati: The Standard Publishing Company, 1918), p. 48.

4. Richardson, Volume II, pp. 107-122.

5. *Ibid,* p. 95.

6. *Ibid,* pp. 94-95.

7. Rogers, *Biography of Stone,* p. 341.

8. Errett Gates, *The Early Relation and Separation of Baptists and Disciples* (Chicago: The Christian Century Company, 1904), p. 69.

9. *Ibid.*

10. *Ibid,* p. 70.

11. *Ibid.*

12. *Ibid.*

13. *Ibid,* pp. 71-72.

14. *Ibid,* p. 72.

15. Frank M. Masters, *A History of the Baptists in Kentucky* (Louisville: Kentucky Baptist Historical Society, 1953), p. 220.

16. *Ibid,* pp. 220-221.

17. J.W. Waldrop, *History of the Concord Association* (Owenton, Ky.: News Herald Print, 1907), p. 6.

18. Masters, p. 221.

19. Walter Lee, *A History of the Elkhorn Baptist Association.* This is a small, unnumbered booklet, but by count this is on pp. 8, 9.

20. Masters, pp. 221-222.

21. John Rogers, *The Biography of Elder J.T. Johnson* (Nashville: Gospel Advocate Company, 1956), pp. 25,26.

22. Ward Russell, *Church Life in the Blue Grass,* 1783-1933, p. 33. This book contains no information regarding its publication.

23. Masters, p. 222.

24. *Ibid,* p. 217.

25. *Ibid.*

26. *Ibid,* pp. 217-218.

27. Alexander Campbell, "Associations, Proscriptions and Anathemas," *The Millennial Harbinger,* Volume I (September 6, 1830), pp. 416-418.

28. Murch, *Christians Only,* p. 110.

29. "Life and Times of John Rogers, of Carlisle, Ky.," Southern Historical Collection, Chapel Hill, p. 66.

30. Rogers, *John Smith,* pp. 353, 358.

31. *Ibid,* p. 354.

32. Murch, pp. 114-119, gives an excellent summary of the differences.

33. "Life and Times of John Rogers," pp. 95-96.

34. John Rogers, *Autobiography of Elder Samuel Rogers* (Cincinnati: Standard Publishing Company, 1909), pp. 55-56.

35. *Ibid,* p. 56.

36. B.F. Hall is an example of this. See *Ibid,* pp. 57-59.

37. Rogers, *John Smith,* p. 358.

38. Barton W. Stone, "The Millennial Harbinger," *The Christian Messenger,* Volume IV (December, 1830), p. 272.

39. Barton W. Stone, "Remarks on A. Campbell's Reply on Union, Communion and the Name Christian," *The Christian Messenger,* Volume V (November, 1831), p. 252.

40. Barton W. Stone, "Reply," *The Christian Messenger,* Volume IV (September, 1830), p. 235.

41. Barton W. Stone, (No heading), *The Christian Messenger,* Volume IV (September, 1830), p. 229.

42. Mrs. N.E. Lamb, corrected and revised by J.F. Burnett, *Autobiography of Abraham Snethen, The Barefoot Preacher* (Dayton: The Christian Publishing Association, 1909), p. 186.

43. Barton W. Stone, "Feet Washing," *The Christian Messenger,* Volume XII (December, 1841), pp. 55-56.

44. For evidence of this, see letter from J.R. Green, Bloomingburg, Ohio, January 9, 1839, in *Christian Palladium,* Volume VII, p. 318, and letter from Adam McCool dated December 15, 1833, in *The Christian Messenger,* Volume VIII (January, 1834), p. 17.

4

DRAWING TOGETHER

INTRODUCTION

Union between two large bodies requires cooperation. Although there was not yet total cooperation of the main leaders, other leaders refused to let the principles which they expounded remain only principles. Union in fact was the goal of many preachers in Ohio, Indiana, Illinois, and Kentucky. The result of the unrelenting drive of these men brought several local unions into existence prior to the larger merger in 1832.

THE WORK ON THE WESTERN RESERVE

The similarities of the Christians and the Reformers played a prominent role in setting the stage for a union. Indeed, without them a union could never have occurred. The greatest praise, however, must be directed to the actors upon the stage, and some of the loudest applause must go to some who were not the stars. While the meeting in Lexington, Kentucky, in January, 1832, is recognized as the time and place that brought the two groups together, similar unions had occurred in a number of communities throughout Ohio, Indiana, Illinois, and Kentucky prior to the Lexington meeting. The importance of these should not be underestimated because they prepared the way for Lexington. Preachers from each group shared their pulpits, meetings, and homes with those of the other group, creating mutual feelings of love, trust, and understanding. Personal fellowship and study, traveling and preaching together, often brought accord in thinking and they led entire congregations together in union. J.E. Church, a Christian minister, wrote from the home of Walter Scott, a Reformer, where he expected "to tarry with him a few days," to Barton Stone asking his opinion regarding some of Scott's views.

> With Elder Walter Scott I fell in company a few days ago, at Fairfield, O. He has made an unusual number of disciples the past year. His method and manner are somewhat novel to me; but in consequence of his extraordinary success in reforming mankind, I feel no disposition at present to pronounce him heretical. He seems to suppose the Apostolical Gospel to consist of the five following particulars, *viz:* faith, repentance, baptism for remission of sins, the gift of the Holy Ghost, and eternal life. Thus you see he baptizes the subject previous to the remission of his sins, or the receiving of the Holy Spirit. . . . He was appointed last year by the Mahoning Association of Baptists to travel, and the development of those peculiar principles of his grew out of that appointment. His general principles correspond very nearly with those which are peculiar to Christians.[1]

Stone, apologizing that he did not have some copies of past issues of the *Messenger* where he had treated the subject, responded,

> We have for some time practised in this way throughout our country. Many of the most successful Baptists pursue the same course. I have

no doubt but that it will become the universal practice, though vehemently opposed.[2]

The focal point for much of the discussion was the teaching of baptism for the remission of sins. While the leaders of the two movements, Stone and Campbell, claimed priority in preaching this doctrine, Walter Scott claimed to have developed it to the point of usefulness.

Scott became the evangelist for the Mahoning Baptist Association at its meeting in New Lisbon, Ohio, on August 23, 1827, when the Braceville church in Trumbull County presented the following petition to the association:

> We wish that this association may take into serious consideration the peculiar situation of the churches of the association, and if it would be a possible thing for an evangelical preacher to be employed to travel and teach among the churches, we think that a blessing would follow.[3]

Thirteen of the sixteen churches had delegates at this meeting[4] and, in addition, three ministers of the Christian Church came: J. Merrill, John Secrest, and Joseph Gaston who by resolution, were "... made equally welcome to the sittings of the association."[5] When the Braceville petition was presented, a committee was appointed to nominate a person as evangelist and suggest a plan for supporting him. The three Christian Church preachers were placed on the committee with the Reformer teachers present. The committee suggested Scott and their entire report was adopted.[6]

Scott immediately entered the field where he developed, presented, and encouraged in practice what had previously been written about and debated, namely baptism for the remission of sins and the gift of the Holy Spirit subsequent to baptism. At the time of the appointment of an evangelist, quarterly meetings were suggested. The first of these met at Braceville during which Adamson Bentley from Warren preached on the subject of baptism for the remission of sins.

Bentley, Scott, Jacob Osborne of Braceville, and Darwin Atwater from Hiram continued discussion of the subject after the meeting. Osborne asked Scott "if he had ever thought that baptism in the name of the Lord was for the remission of sins?"[7] Scott encouraged him to continue expressing his thoughts and when he finished, Scott agreed with him.

> After a little, Mr. Osborne remarked to Elder Bentley, "you have christened baptism to-day." "How so?" "You termed it a remitting ordinance." Bentley replied, "I do not see how we are to avoid the conclusion with the Bible in our hands."[8]

Shortly after this event Scott, Osborne, and Bentley were together again and Osborne preached on the concept that the gift of the Holy Spirit comes after baptism, not before. Scott now began arranging the elements of the gospel as he understood them under six headings of faith, repentance, baptism, remission of sins, the Holy Spirit, and eternal life through a patient continuance in well doing.[9] Hayden states that at this point, "A new era for the gospel had dawned."[10] Scott pointed to this year, 1827, as the time when the "ancient gospel" was restored.

Scott divided the message of the Reformers into two sections; (1) the ancient gospel and (2) the ancient order. The first of these, said Scott, ". . . includes everything in the doctrine of Christ necessary to make disciples," and the second ". . . everything necessary to keep them disciples."[11] In 1832 he listed six items under the ancient gospel; (1) faith, (2) repentance, (3) baptism, (4) remission, (5) Holy Spirit, (6) resurrection, and six items under the ancient order; (1) government, (2) worship, (3) ordinances, (4) discipline, (5) manner and customs, and (6) literature.[12] He claimed that the ancient order of things was initially set down by him and ten or twelve others in 1819 and pointed to his first year as an evangelist on the Western Reserve as the time of restoration of the ancient gospel. Concerning the development of restoring the ancient gospel, Scott wrote,

I had consulted no mortal on the topic of the Ancient Gospel, the very phrase was unknown, except in a single piece, which was dropt from *my own pen* about two or three months before. I was prompted to it by no man nor set of men, nor did I get it from men, but from the book of God, and that too by a course of reading, meditation and prayer to God, which he alone knows, and to him alone the praise is due. My essays on the *one fact* required to be carried out and the matter of them reduced to practice.

In my very first tour, I left the association ground, went to the one side and made an unsuccessful experiment of the Ancient Gospel: the people fled, but I renewed the experiment with success shortly afterwards, in another place, and actually immersed the converts for the remission of sins, and for the Holy Spirit spoken by Peter, Acts 2nd. Nothing however as yet had been published on the subject of the Ancient Gospel.

All was at present *experiment,* had no model but the Apostles; had seen no mortal immerse for the remission of sins, no man accept the candidate, on the simple confession of the *'one fact,'* no person propose that believers should be baptized, that they might receive the Holy Spirit.

I proceeded in this matter without example, without council, and without reference to any mode or practice which I ever saw or ever heard of. I followed Christ and his apostles alone, and the experiment was crowned with complete success.[13]

This event occurred in November, 1827, "from which moment the whole country around, preachers and people, were aroused, and all illuminated; all was bustle confusion and conversion."[14]

The ancient gospel became the focal point of the preaching and, through the writings of Campbell and the preaching of Scott, probably was the principal factor in the revival fervor that characterized the late 1820's and early 1830's as the possibilities for union became realities. It also produced the greatest amount of controversy surrounding the union.[15]

Armed with the ancient gospel and the ancient order, Scott labored among the churches on the Western Reserve, then into other parts of Ohio, serving not only as an evangelist, but as a catalyst between the Reformers and the Christians. The two bodies united together in several areas, and regardless of who may have been the first to preach immersion for remission of sins, the Reformer churches were more advanced in this doctrine than the Christians, and forbearance was necessary by the Reformers until the Christians could be fully persuaded.

Joseph Gaston, whom Scott assigned the position of being first among the Christian preachers "who received the gospel after its restoration and who argued for the remission of sins by baptism,"[16] became a traveling companion of Scott. He took Scott to some of the Christian Churches on the Western Reserve, where "whole churches of the 'New Lights' (Christians) and of the Baptists (Reformers), in Salem, New Lisbon, East Fairfield, Green, New Garden, Hanover, and Minerva . . . became one people in the Lord and in his work."[17] Gaston soon became ill and another Christian preacher, James G. Mitchell, accompanied Scott for the rest of the year.[18] Because of a spirit of co-operation between the two groups, other Christian preachers joined with the Reformers in Ohio very near this time, namely John Whitacre, William Schooley, John Flick,[19] Joseph Pancoast, Lewis Hamrick, Lewis Comer,[20] and James Hughes.[21]

Hayden gives accounts of situations in three communities on the Western Reserve where the two groups united into one body: East Fairfield, Fairfield, and Canfield. Scott, accompanied by Mitchell, preached at East Fairfield for ten days which resulted in "thirty-seven additions, all new converts, beside instructing many of the old Christian order in more scriptural views of the gospel, especially in regard to the design of baptism."[22]

The Christians were the predominant group in Columbiana County, showing the extent of the influence of the Christians. Joseph Gaston preached at one of the large churches, located at Fairfield. Gaston and Scott visited among the Christians of this community, conversing freely on the subject of the ancient gospel. Scott then spoke at the church on the "master key of Peter, Pentecost, and pardon."

> The theme was new, and in his hands the scriptural scheme of the gospel was so plain and convincing, scarcely a doubt was left in the great audience. At the close of his sermon, the proposition was made to take the sense of the church upon the overture now submitted, to assume the position of a gospel church, in accordance with the scriptural teaching they had just heard. There was almost a unanimous rising up. Only five or six refused.[23]

The import of this account seems to be that the Christians came over to the views of the Reformers on the doctrine of baptism for remission of sins. Other communities where these men brought the two bodies together were Salem, New Lisbon, Green, New Garden, Hanover, and Minerva.[24]

Canfield provides another illustration where the Christians seemed to join the Reformers. William Schooley ministered to the Christians and William Hayden was appointed minister of the Reformers in 1828.

> These two churches — the "Christians" and the Disciples — became better acquainted, and Br. Schooley himself having united with the Disciples in Salem, these communities united as one brotherhood in Christ; thus giving practical illustration of the union and co-operation of Christians on the original foundation . . . about twenty were enrolled with the Disciples, as one people in Christ.[25]

Accounts of individuals from the Christian Church uniting with the Reformer churches indicates a harmonious spirit between the two groups on the Western Reserve. One such example is the Dougald McDougall family uniting with the Reformers to constitute the church at Royalton, which selected him as one of the deacons.[26]

Charles Loos, a preacher with personal knowledge of the Western Reserve, gives an excellent summation of the interworkings of the two bodies in Eastern Ohio and Pennsylvania.

> Wherever in our earlier days the "Christians" came into close acquaintance with the "Disciples," the name by which those in sym-

pathy with the Bethany movement were generally called, . . . a sympathy at once grew up between them. The effect was that in Eastern Ohio and in Pennsylvania, without any formal action, many of the former, not only individuals, but entire congregations, led by the preachers, coalesced with the latter, and the two became permanently one.

I am familiar with this territory and its religious history, and can speak advisedly; hardly a "Christian" congregation was left out of the union in Eastern Ohio.[27]

OTHER PARTS OF OHIO

The amalgamation of the two bodies was not as complete in southeastern Ohio as on the Reserve. Stone had preached in Meigs County around 1815 and immersed William Caldwell, a Presbyterian minister. This caught the attention of the Baptists who invited Stone to speak at their annual meeting on the subject of church government. Stone accepted and made an appeal for Christian unity in his message resulting in about twelve elders agreeing to

. . . throw away their name Baptist, and take the name Christian — and to bury their association, and to become one with us in the great work of Christian union. They then marched up in a band to the stand, shouting the praise of God, and proclaiming aloud what they had done. We met them, and embraced each other with Christian love, by which the union was cemented.[28]

Meigs County, it seems, served as the tie for the Kentucky preachers of the Christian group to the Reformers in eastern Ohio and Virginia as they traveled into Guernsey and Belmont Counties, then into Stark, Carroll, and Columbiana Counties where they came in close contact with the Reformers. The most important of these men to the development of this relationship was John Secrest, the preacher Campbell credited with first preaching the doctrine of baptism for the remission of sins in its practicality.

Secrest moved from Kentucky in 1826, focusing attention

upon Belmont, Harrison, Guernsey, Monroe, and Columbiana Counties. He enjoyed going to Bethany for visits with Alexander Campbell who persuaded him on the subject of baptism for remission of sins. He began immediately to preach the doctrine among the Christians in eastern and southeastern Ohio, immersing at least three thousand converts in two years. In 1827 he baptized Nathan Mitchell who subsequently made a major contribution to the fraternity of the two bodies.[29]

Traveling toward Cincinnati in 1829 to hear the debate between Campbell and Robert Owen, Nathan and his brother, James Mitchell, preached in Morgan, Athens, and Meigs Counties stirring revivals in the churches. Entering Meigs County they came in contact with two of the Christian preachers, B.H. Miles, who preached at Rutland, and William Caldwell, Stone's old convert. The Christian Churches in this area evidently had not previously accepted or known firsthand of the teaching of baptism for the remission of sins that was rapidly becoming an accepted doctrine among the churches and were still accustomed to the use of the mourner's bench. Miles obviously witnessed this new doctrine in practice as his own sister responded to the gospel and when she was immersed Miles leaned over to Nathan Mitchell and said, "I do not know whether this is right or not; but, at any rate, baptize all you can."[30] How much effect this had on Caldwell is unknown, but he later moved to Bedford County, Pennsylvania, where he joined the Reformers. The Meigs County churches had problems following the Kentucky union of the two bodies, but in 1829 a spirit of co-operation did exist between the two bodies. As the Mitchells moved on toward Cincinnati they preached at Deer Creek where James Burbridge ministered, and after several sermons the congregation ". . . appeared to receive the 'ancient gospel' with all readiness." Burbridge later joined the reformation.[31]

Union and a spirit of co-operation prevailed in southern

and southwestern Ohio also. Two churches in Brown County provide one example of union; Liberty Chapel, a Reformed Baptist church with Jesse Holton as their preacher, and the Christian Church at Red Oak under the ministerial leadership of John Longley and David Hathaway united together into one body. No date is affixed to this except that it occurred prior to 1832.[32]

A co-operative attitude prevailed at Georgetown where the Christian Church began in 1826, providing the base four years later for communion with the Reformers in their assemblies. One of the new converts wrote to Stone, "We have the satisfaction of seeing some of our brethren and sisters of different denominations (particularly the Reformed Baptists) commune with us."[33] The burden for Christian union, he added, was at the center of almost every prayer, the theme of conversations, and ". . . the subject of frequent meditation with the members of the church of Christ, with whom I am acquainted in this state."[34] While a state of harmony prevailed in Georgetown, he closed his communication citing a problem to possible union of the two bodies in other places.

> I believe that the Christians, and the Reformers among the Baptist brethren, would unite in many places were it not for the preachers. I did intend giving an instance of a proposed union, which was objected to by a Reforming preacher; but . . . my sheet is almost exhausted.[35]

Samuel Rogers became a vital link between the two groups in his early labors centered in Clinton County, Ohio. Samuel joined the Concord Church in Kentucky in 1817 and began preaching immediately. He moved his family to Clinton County in September, 1818, and began preaching to a small group which he gathered together at Hester's school house on Todd's Fork. This group later erected the first building of the Christian Church in that sector, naming it Antioch.[36]

Samuel and his brother, John, traced their religious roots to the Stone movement but were greatly influenced by Campbell. Exactly how this influence grew is not totally known, but pieces can be placed together with some degree of accuracy. John Rogers first heard Campbell preach on December 6, 1825, at Carlisle, Kentucky, and purchased three volumes of *The Christian Baptist,*[37] apparently his first exposure to the man and his teachings. Approximately eighteen months later Samuel and John united together for a three-months tour of Virginia, Pennsylvania, and Ohio, during which there seemed to be an insatiable desire to learn all they could about Campbell and his teachings.[38]

Arriving at Charlotte Court-house, Virginia, they stayed with their kinsman, John Roach, a Baptist preacher, who introduced them to A.W. Clopton, also a Baptist preacher, but a subscriber to *The Christian Baptist* who had some knowledge of Campbell's views. This excited the brothers who listened ". . . with eager interest to everything we could hear about Alexander Campbell, for already we had been catching glimpses of light sufficient to stimulate our desire for more."[39] At the end of the two-week stay with Roach, the brothers parted company as John headed through Virginia toward Bethany ". . . with the intention of spending a few days with Brother Campbell, that he might get from his own lips what were his views upon certain questions that had recently disturbed and bewildered his mind."[40] As Samuel traveled he questioned others about Campbell's views, gathering information from different preachers, including a Brother Fife in Fredricksburg, Virginia, Brother Winebrenner in Harrisburg, Pennsylvania, and in Ohio from John Secrest and John Whitacre.[41] From what information he had gathered and the scant reading of Campbell's writings which he could get, Samuel longed for the opportunity to hear Campbell personally. Again, piecing together the available information, he had the opportunity at Wilmington, Ohio, shortly after this trip which led to serious study in his congregation.[42]

> Most of the members of the Antioch church, where I had my membership, now betook themselves to a careful and prayerful study of the word of God, such as I had never witnessed before. The result was, that with a few exceptions, they were in a short time willing to adopt the apostolic order of things, as to church government and worship. There were a few brethren who could not see their way clear to observe the ordinance of the Lord's Supper upon every first day of the week. They, however, with a spirit of becoming liberality, were not inclined to put any obstacle in the way of the majority who felt it to be their duty to so observe it.[43]

Within a little over a year the church was completely structured after the ideas of Campbell in respect to the ancient order.

The Antioch Church had a far-reaching impact.

> Like Antioch of old, the gospel movement went out from this center to Clinton, Darke, Highland, Brown, Clermont, and other counties, and furnished centers from which churches grew up and into the fullness of the Restoration movement. Great credit should be given to the Christian denomination for paving the way for complete New Testament faith and practice.[44]

Samuel Rogers provided an essential bridging between the Christians and the Reformers in that section of Ohio, but the important role that his brother played in creating the stage for union was no less significant. John was a contributor to *The Christian Messenger* and a close friend to Stone, yet possessing a thirst to learn that led him to an investigation of the ideas of Campbell through reading and personal conversation. He provided another link between the two bodies in Kentucky. He had, by December, 1830, embraced the doctrine of baptism for the remission of sins,[45] recording the following in his journal,

> Our views of Baptism for remission of sins, & of the Breaking of bread every Lord's, &c appear to us very clearly taught in the Christian

Scriptures; yet our honest opposers, from the influence of false systems, — of causes over which they have had no control, are unprepared to receive them; as unprepared as many of us were ourselves a few years ago.[46]

Ohio furnished a field for vital contact between the Reformers and Christians where the doctrinal development and practice of baptism for remission of sins provided a focal point that drew them closer together. Secrest, from the Christians, and Scott, from the Reformers, if we are to believe the abundance of testimony, must have almost simultaneously, yet separately, developed the matter and experienced great success in proclaiming it. Contact with other preachers, particularly those of the Christian background, with these men in eastern Ohio helped to spread this teaching, as did the ensuing writings of Campbell.[47] Ohio provided the seedbed for the doctrine to find development, which in turn provided a topic for discussion in the two journals that must be given priority for drawing them together.

INDIANA

While Ohio provided some examples of union, the groups in Indiana provided further illustration to their brethren in Kentucky of the possibilities of union. John Wright heads the list of those who labored for union on the principles of the Bible alone, succeeding in 1819 in persuading the Baptists at Blue River to take the name of Christ upon them instead of the name Baptist. Other Baptist churches in the area followed with the same action, also making their association meetings into annual meetings for worship and fellowship.[48] Wright then proposed at the annual meeting in either 1821 or 1822 that they send a letter requesting Christian union to the Tunkers who had fifteen congregations in the area. The Tunkers had just undergone a controversy over triune immersion, and the single-immersionist group led by Abram Kern and Peter Hon succeeded in getting their position adopted, placing the Tunkers on a similar platform with the Reformed Baptists. The Tunkers accepted the proposal and union resulted.[49]

Wright made the same proposition to the Christian Churches in the area,[50] and union came in 1828. Wright, his brother, Peter, and about six other elders of this group, identified as "Depending Baptists" formerly, united with the Christian Churches at their conference. The correspondent for the conference reported:

> When we met in conference together, we could find nothing to separate us asunder. — In fine, we saw as nearly eye to eye as any company of elders who have assembled in modern times — and then there was such a sweet spirit of love. I shall never forget this meeting. We abounded in brotherly love. We were almost as cautious of wounding one another's feelings as if we had been in our father's own country.[51]

Others sources say that Beverly Vawter spoke for the Christians and Wright for the Baptists on this occasion.[52] Only one church refused to enter the union and it soon died out.

Wright now turned some of his attention toward the Reformers of the area, namely those among the Silver Creek Baptist Association. Several of the preachers in this body, namely Absolem and John Littell, and Mordecai Cole, espoused the views of Alexander Campbell, creating some serious controversy. Hundreds of individuals, sometimes entire congregations, voted out their articles of faith and took the position of the Reformers. While a proximity of views existed between this group and the united Christian Church, each feared union with the other might bring a stigma upon it; the Reformers fearing the name of Arians and the Christians fearful of being termed Campbellites. Wright broke the stalemate by establishing communication between the two groups. They found they preached nearly the same doctrines except on the subject of baptism for the remission of sins. Wright came over to this position as a result of these investigations and succeeded in bringing a permanent union together, aided by his brother Peter, Abraham Kern, Mordecai Cole, and the Littells. It is estimated that nearly 3,000 people were united together in this union.[53]

A singular situation, that due to the locale may have been incorporated into the previous union later, occurred in Rush County, Indiana, at Flat Rock. John Thompson led a group of about sixty Reformers out of the Flat Rock Baptist Church sometime after 1826 and organized a Church of Christ. On the following Sunday after organization, Joseph Thomas, an evangelist for the Christian Church, was present and requested to preach. Some Christians from the Christian Church about two miles north were present, but were offended because they were not invited to participate in the Lord's Supper. John Longley, the preacher for the Christians, and Thompson discussed this fervently, but finally the matter was "amicably adjusted," and "Elder Longley with the majority of his brethren soon came over to the Reformation . . ."[54] When Campbell and Stone were engaged in discussing some controversial issues in their respective periodicals, Longley[55] wrote to Stone, informing him that in the last year he had constituted three churches and that he worked with Thompson in constituting two more. His letter closed with this paragraph:

> The Reforming Baptists and we, are all one here, and we hope that the dispute between you and brother Campbell about names and priority, will forever cease, and that you go on united to reform the world. The King will reward each according to your works.[56]

Soon after the doctrine of baptism for the remission of sins became a prominent doctrine among the preachers in

Ohio, it spread to Indiana and played a role in drawing the two groups into a closer relationship. Beverly Vawter, the spokesman for the Christians at the union meeting in 1828, claimed he preached baptism for the remission of sins in 1828,[57] and it probably goes without question that the Reformers were preaching it by this time as a result of Campbell advocating it in *The Christian Baptist* very strongly in early 1828. By 1830 a Christian preacher wrote to Stone, indicating that some of them were accepting it.

> The doctrine of Immersion for the remission of sins, is gaining ground in this country. — Some few of our preaching brethren are, with boldness, proclaiming the ancient gospel. Within a few days, brother Combs and myself have immersed nine or ten in this neighborhood.[58]

Elijah Martindale, a Christian Church preacher, admitted that for ten years he preached that faith, repentance, and prayer were the only divinely appointed means on the sinner's part for forgiveness of sins before preaching baptism for remission.[59] When he first preached this at New Lisbon, Indiana, the congregation was displeased, and "a few of the leading spirits went to work" to stop him. The majority voted they would not tolerate the doctrine in their meetinghouse, but aided by some Reformed Baptists and the minority he was able to continue.

> By careful, kind management we finally overcame the opposition and got nearly all the old members and some of the Baptists united and harmoniously organized on the principles of the reformation.[60]

Some other instances occurred where Christian Churches accepted the doctrine of Campbell and reorganized the church on that basis, including Old Union under James Mathes[61] and a congregation in Lawrence County, Illinois, just over the border, who in 1828, "came fully to apostolic grounds."[62]

KENTUCKY

The Christian Church in Kentucky could also point to some successful union ventures prior to 1832. The annual meeting group to which Stone belonged, the North Conference, meeting at Antioch in Bourbon County on September 19, 1828, received a letter from the Baptized Church at Cooper's Run, informing the Christian Churches of their position and that their "pulpits, meetinghouse, and tables were open" to the Christians.[63] The Conference appointed T.M. Allen and John Rogers to convey the willingness of the Christians to fellowship with the Baptized Church at Cooper's Run. Additional correspondence occurred at the next meeting of the North Conference,[64] and ultimately a full union prevailed, the Cooper's Run Church being listed under the Bourbon County Christian Churches in 1830.[65]

In the area of Columbia County in Southern Kentucky, Jacob Warner, a minister among the South Kentucky Association of Separate Baptists, left that group, relinquishing "his former views of the doctrine of Universalism together with his name and creed" and united with the Christians and started two Christian Churches; Liberty and Harricane Creek. In addition, seven Baptist Churches, some regular and some separate, "have also renounced all party names and creeds, and have taken the name Christian. Several preachers have united with them on these principles."[66] This was reported to Stone by two different Christian Church preachers, James Evans and John Longley.

Union also occurred near the end of 1830 at Beaver Creek Christian Church in Harrison County. Adam Vickery of the Christian Church wrote to Stone, informing him that his mind had undergone an entire revolution on the subject of baptism, and after having studied Barkly, a Friend Quaker, and Mr. Campbell, he viewed Campbell's teaching to be true and was immersed. "Some small difficulties occurred," he wrote, "on the subject of Baptism; but my Brethren were very tender and kind towards me, and I am glad to say, by the Grace of God I hope, that difficulty will be now forever buried."[67] Obviously he and the church had, for the most part, accepted immersion, which probably was the key to the union he reported.

> A union has been lately formed between the separate Baptist Church and the Christian Church at Beaver Creek Meeting-house. The former have taken the name *Christian;* they have united on the word of God, and agreed to have no other rule but what is found written in that Book.[68]

Millersburg, in Bourbon County, had a Christian Church, started by Barton W. Stone in 1820, and a Reformer Church, started by Robert M. Batson. According to the church record union prevailed there.

> It was the practice of the brethren forming the two congregations to commune together at their several meetings, and finally finding themselves to be one so far as faith and practice was concerned they agreed to meet together without any regard to differences of opinion, acknowledging no name but that of Christian, and no creed but the Bible. The result of these joint meetings was a union into one congregation in the year of 1831. . . .[69]

The consummation of this occurred on the fourth Lord's Day, April, 1831.

THE CAMPBELL-STONE CORRESPONDENCE

The foregoing sketches of achieved union and harmonious

relationships existing in a four-state area demonstrated to the leaders, Stone and Campbell, their principles for union were workable. Obviously, however, no larger union would occur without the positive involvement of the leaders. Permitting their stated differences to hinder union would be admission that the principles they advocated so widely were impracticable and impractical.

Stone made the first public overture for a union through the pages of *The Christian Messenger* in September, 1829.

> Not many days ago I was asked by a worthy Baptist brother this important question: Why do not you, as a people, and the New Testament Baptists unite as one people? By the New Testament Baptists he meant those who reject all human creeds as authoritative, and who are generally disposed to receive the name *Christian* to the rejection of all others.[70]

Stone promised to answer this in the *Messenger* and replied:

> I know of no reason, according to scripture, why all *Christians* of every name should not unite as one people. The New Testament enjoins it upon all in the most solemn and express terms. That this is the will of God — the prayer of Jesus — the labor of the apostles — and the design of the gospel, no man in this enlightened day can deny.[71]

He said that some differences of opinion may exist, but as long as these do not lead to irreligion, forbearance should be the rule. The cause of division, he contended, existed in carnality. "Had we all followed after the spirit, division had never been known among Christians. Until we thus walk after the spirit, in vain do we expect and pray for union; . . ."[72] He used his final comments to praise the Reformers.

> The New Testament reformers among the Baptists have generally acted on the part which we approve. They have rejected all party names and have taken the denomination *Christian;* so have we. They

allow each other to read the Bible, and judge its meaning for themselves; so do we. They will not bind each other to believe certain dogmas as terms of fellowship; nor do we. In fact, if there is a difference between us, we know it not. We have nothing in us to prevent a union; and if they have nothing in them in opposition to it, we are in spirit one. May God strengthen the ends of Christian union.[73]

Campbell made no response to this article in his periodical.

Some very strong ties began to grow between some of the Christians and the Reformers in the Lexington area, particularly at Georgetown where Stone preached. Great Crossings, a Reformer Church served by John T. Johnson, was a very short distance from Georgetown and the two men became close friends, sharing a similar passion for unity, and agreeing to promote a wider unity among the two bodies.[74] With such prospects before them, Stone used the pages of the *Messenger* to again stir some support for union between the two groups, once more taking the initiative in the August, 1831, issue.

The question is going the round of society, and is often proposed to us, Why are not you and the Reformed Baptists one people? or, Why are you not united? We have uniformly answered; In spirit we are united, and that no reason existed on our side to prevent the union in form. It is well known to those brethren, and to the world, that we have always, from the beginning, declared our willingness, and desire to be united with the whole family of God on earth, irrespective of the diversity of opinion among them. The Reformed Baptists have received the doctrine taught by us many years ago. For nearly 30 years we have taught that Sectarianism was anti-christian, and that all christians should be united in the one body of Christ — the same they teach. We *then* and ever since, have taught that authoritative creeds and confessions were the strong props of sectarianism, and should be given to the moles and the bats — they teach the same. We have from that time preached the gospel to every creature to whom we had access, and urged them to believe and obey it — that its own evidence was sufficient to produce faith in all that heard it, that the unrenewed sinner must, and could believe it unto justification and salvation — and that through faith the Holy Spirit of promise, and every other promise of the New Covenant were given. They proclaim the same doctrine. Many years ago some of us preached baptism as a means, in connexion with faith and repentance, for the remission of sins, and the gift of the Holy Spirit — they preach the same, and extend it farther than we have done. We rejected all names, but Christian — they acknowledge it most proper, but seem to prefer another. We acknowledge a difference of opinion from them on some points. We do not object to their opinions as terms of fellowship between us. But they seriously and honestly object to some of ours as reasons why they cannot unite.[75]

The significant objections, Stone believed, were (1) the Christians would participate in the Lord's Supper with the unimmersed and would permit the unimmersed to participate with them, and (2) preference for the name, "Disciple," over "Christian" by some of the Reformers. He discussed his position at length on these two items, adding in the theme of immersion for the remission of sins. He stated:

We are ready any moment, to meet and unite with these brethren, or any others, who believe in, and obey the Saviour according to their best understanding of his will, on the Bible, but not on opinions of its truth. We cannot with our present views unite on the opinion that unimmersed persons cannot receive the remission of their sins, and therefore should be excluded from our fellowship and communion on earth. We cannot conscientiously give up the name *Christian,* acknowledged by our brethren most appropriate, for any other (as *Disciple*) less appropriate, and received to avoid the disgrace of being suspected to be a Unitarian or Trinitarian. We cannot thus temporize with divine truth.[76]

Many of the "speculations" that had created some earlier conflicts between Campbell and Stone and some of their disciples, seemed now to disappear into the background as minor items. In practice, they were nearly identical, but, in theory, differences still existed.[77] Stone and the other leading Christian preachers in the area had accepted the practice of the weekly communion, but would not make it a binding matter upon those who saw differently. They observed the Supper regularly, but, in Stone's terms, neither invited nor debarred anyone from the table, thus permitting the unimmersed to partake. Immersion for the remission of sins was their normal practice, but Stone would not rule out God's grace to those who had not accepted this or ever heard it. The name seemed to be no barrier for the Kentucky Reformers, since some of those who had united with the Christians prior to this in Kentucky had graciously accepted that terminology. Apparently the article was intended to create a spirit of inquiry and open discussion for what was about to develop in this area of the country, but the depth of the discourse to support the positions of the Christians suggests that he was making a larger appeal than this; apparently to Alexander Campbell, who printed the entire article and then reviewed it in the September issue of the *Millennial Harbinger.*

Campbell questioned how Stone would propose such a union to happen in their circumstances and invited him to propose a more definitive view. After suggesting that he thought Stone was "squinting at some sort of precedency or priority . . . which are perhaps only in appearance, and not in reality;"[78] Campbell turned to what he considered the real issue; not what Stone's group stood against thirty years ago — creeds, councils, and other abuses — but the ground on which the Reformers presently stood. Many groups, Campbell chortled, had stood against these things, some of them the greatest of all heretics. But the present cause of reformation had different objectives.

> Both friends and foes of the cause which we now plead, seem to be agreed that not the anti-creed, and anti-council, and anti-sectarian questions, but what may be denominated the questions of the "ancient gospel and ancient order of things," distinguish it most easily from every other cause plead on this continent or in Europe since the great apostasy. Not, indeed, because it has not some things in common with other causes; but because when all the common things are taken into the account, it presents what some of our opponents call a new religion — an exhibit of christianity as different from the sectarian as Protestantism differs from Popery; and if I were to give my opinion, I would say, much more different.
>
> I trust our brother Editor will not think that we are merely

disputing his claims to priority, as it is not assumed by us that he has set up such a claim; but only that in appearance it squints that way: but that he will consider us as endeavoring to prevent the confounding of the *ancient gospel* and *ancient order of things* with the anti-creed, or anti-council, or anti-sectarian cause. Sorry would I be to think that any would be so indiscriminating as to identify the principles of this reformation with the principles of any other reformation preached since Luther was born.[79]

Campbell viewed his reformation as completely different from any other in history, although in its beginning, it too was anti-credal, anti-council, and anti-sectarian. By 1831, however, his reformation stood on new ground; the ancient gospel and the ancient order of things were its themes.

For our part, we might be honored much by a union formal and public, with a society so large and so respectable as the Christian denomination; but if our union with them, though so advantageous to us, would merge "the ancient gospel and ancient order of things" in the long vexed questions of simple anti-trinitarianism, anti-creedism, or anti-sectarianism, I should be ashamed of myself in the presence of him whose *"well done, good and faithful servant,"* is worth the universe to me. We all could have had honorable alliances with honorable sectaries, many years since, had this been our object.[80]

Guarding his remarks closely, Campbell confessed his high respect for Stone and brethren with him, but avoided a blanket approval of all the Christians, stating, "Many of them with whom we are acquainted we love as brethren; and we can, in all good conscience, unite with them in spirit and form, in public or in private, in all acts of social worship."[81]

Stone thought that Campbell's reply in the *Millennial Harbinger* somewhat out of character. He responded in the November issue of his paper, implying in his opening remarks that Campbell was a hindrance to unity, hinting that Campbell had designs on building a great name. Stone wrote,

I once heard an old Baptist preacher say, that the enemies to Christian Union, were the world, the flesh, and the Devil; and I will add, said he, the fourth, more mischievous than all, the preachers. The remark is humiliating to this class of christians, and willingly would I prove it false. Since that time the impression has remained indelible on my mind, and to good effect. I am aware of the deceptibility of the human mind, and of its strong propensity to make for ourselves a *great name.* This was the spirit of the builders of ancient Babylon, and figuratively, the church in her apostacy is called Babylon, because possessed of the same spirit. Until this proud spirit sink at the feet of Jesus, and we become cordially and joyfully willing to decrease, that Christ may increase, I cannot anticipate as near that happy period of the church, so much talked of and prayed for at this time. Great zeal is manifested, and great exertions are made to advance religion, and great effects too, are produced; but so little of apostolic religion is seen, and I fear the zeal, the exertions, and the products all lack the divine impress of heaven. So long have the clergy stood in the way of truth's advancement — so long and so often have the preachers divided those whom God had joined together by the spirit of truth, that I am afraid of myself, and jealous of others. I would rather my hand were palsied, than that it should direct a pen to any of these unhallowed purposes.[82]

There seems to be little question that Campbell is the main subject of this indictment. Stone wrote that Campbell misunderstood what he had written on the subject and defended his remarks and responded to those of Campbell.

Campbell recognized the implications of Stone, responding in the December, 1831, issue of the *Millennial Harbinger,* stating that he feared their discussions, instead of tending to union, will tend to disunion. Campbell felt hurt by Stone's reply, obviously not giving any thought to the remarks he had made regarding Stone in his first response. He implied that if his remarks were in the spirit that he detected in Stone's article that "many would regret that he had noticed his writings at all on the subject."[83] He openly expressed his displeasure with Stone's comments.

It is true I feel displeased with some unkind *insinuations* in the piece before me, and some uncandid remarks, as I apprehend them, because they weaken my regard for the writer, which I would not have impaired for the whole controversy. Until he explain, in a satisfactory manner, the reasons why he insinuates that I am, or was, in my remarks, influenced by "the propensity to make for myself a *great name,*" and actuated by "a proud spirit," I can make no reply to the piece before me. He must be dull of apprehension who sees not that such insinuations are made in the very commencement of the piece alluded to.[84]

Campbell remarked that he expected a better spirit from those who claimed to be Christians and that he would solicit a free, candid and affectionate correspondence on differences. He thought he had "treated most delicately, for years, their sectarian peculiarities" and now he rejoiced to see that "many of them in the *West* are fast advancing in the knowledge of the christian scriptures."[85] He praised the Christians as a people.

But in Kentucky, and the South-West generally, . . . many of the congregations called "Christians" are just as sound in the faith of Jesus as the only begotten son of God, in the plain import of these terms, as any congregations with which I am acquainted. With all such, I, as an individual, am united, and would rejoice in seeing all the immersed disciples of the Son of God, called "Christians," and walking in all the commandments of the Lord and Saviour. We plead for the union, communion, and co-operation of all such; and wherever there are in any vicinity a remnant of those who keep the commandments of Jesus, whatever may have been their former designation, they ought to rally under Jesus and the Apostles, and bury all dissensions about such unprofitable questions as those long vexed questions about trinity, atonement, depravity, election, effectual calling, &c. . . . With all such I am united in heart and in hand, and with all such I will, with the help of God, co-operate in any measure which can conduce to the furtherance of the gospel of Christ.[86]

Was Campbell attempting to appeal to the Christians for a union while side-stepping Stone? Some historians have taken that view from these remarks and such a conclusion is not without warrant. Campbell had seen some of the Christian preachers accept his positions regarding the ancient gospel, some congregations on the Western Reserve came together without any cooperation from Stone, and he may have had high aspirations for a union of the two bodies as the Christians flowed toward him.

Had Stone not taken the lead the union would not have occurred when it did. The fellowship between Stone and Johnson, drawing in Smith and Rogers, created an atmosphere for union in Kentucky in which Campbell had no main part. Stone and Johnson encouraged their members to respect one another and worship together, and, while Campbell and Stone had some previous conversations about a possible union of the two bodies, the practical arrangement, seems to have originated with these two men who "plainly saw that there was no scriptural barrier to their union."[87]

Johnson sent for John Smith to come to Great Crossing for a meeting in November, 1831. The Christians attended this meeting, and when it concluded Stone, Smith, Johnson, and John Rogers of Carlisle held a private conference. "The subject of a general union of the churches was discussed, its importance and practicability were admitted, and the time and manner of effecting it were considered."[88] They decided on a course of action, concluding that two meetings, close together, would be an effective procedure. They set the dates; the first would be a four-day meeting at Georgetown "embracing Christmas day and afterward" and the second would begin on New Year's day, 1832, at Lexington. Invitations were sent to members of both groups to attend.[89]

CHAPTER SUMMARY

Numerous unions between the Reformers and Christians occurred prior to 1832 that set the stage for the larger union in Kentucky. The primary force behind these unions was local preachers who worked diligently to effect them. On the Western Reserve in Ohio Walter Scott and a number of Christian Church preachers traveled and preached together, bringing a spirit of unity into that part of the state. The largest group, perhaps as many as 3,000, united in Indiana, while some of the Christian Churches there accepted the doctrines of Campbell and reorganized upon that basis without necessarily merging with Reformers in the same community. Illinois and Kentucky provided some examples of local unions. Still the "sparrings" between the two editors, Stone and Campbell, hung as a dark cloud over the prospects of union.

1. Barton W. Stone, "Extract of a letter from Elder J.E. Church," *The Christian Messenger,* Volume II (September, 1828), p. 261.

2. Stone, "Answers to Bro: Church's Remarks," *The Christian Messenger,* Volume II (September, 1828), p. 262.

3. A.S. Hayden, *Early History of the Disciples in the Western Reserve, Ohio* (Cincinnati: Chase and Hall, Publishers, 1875), p. 57.

4. Wilcox, *History of the Disciples,* pp. 49-50.

5. Hayden, p. 57.

6. *Ibid,* pp. 57-58.

7. *Ibid,* pp. 69-70.

8. *Ibid,* p. 70.

9. *Ibid,* p. 71.

10. *Ibid.*

11. Walter Scott, "The Reformation," *The Evangelist,* Volume I (January, 1832), p. 93.

12. Walter Scott, "Three Divine Institutions," *The Evangelist,* Volume I (April, 1832), p. 93.

13. *Ibid,* p. 94.

14. *Ibid,* p. 95.

15. Some questions arose over the statements of Scott in regard to the origin of the restoration of the ancient gospel. He contended that he wrote to Campbell on January 4, 1828, telling him about the events cited, then contends that Campbell issued his first piece on the subject in the January 7, 1828, issue. Scott's letter was not published in *The Christian Baptist* until the February, 1828, issue, and very possibly did not get into Campbell's hands until after the issue of the paper was printed. It is still quite possible that Campbell had heard orally about Scott's preaching and the results before he received the letter. Campbell, however, had stated in the December issue that he had an essay prepared on the ancient gospel, but lacked space for it. (Volume V, p. 123) It commanded the first few pages of the January, 1828, issue. Two matters of interest, however, appear in this essay. First, Campbell cited his debate with McCalla in 1823 as the place where he contended that "Immersion in water into the name of the Father, Son, and Holy Spirit . . . was a divine institution designed for putting the legitimate subject of it in actual possession of the remission of his sins — that to every believing subject it did *formally,* and *in fact,* convey to him the forgiveness of sins." (Volume V, p. 128) He said he presented the view with hesitation because of its perfect novelty. However, he was assured of its truth, he stated, but had now given more serious consideration to the subject and was better prepared to develop its import. The second item of significance in the essay was that Campbell had hosted John Secrest, one of the Christian preachers who had been given a seat at the Mahoning Association, in his home on November 23, 1827, and stated that over the past five months Secrest had immersed nearly five hundred people, "... for it is not more than five months since he began to proclaim the gospel and christian immersion in its primitive simplicity and import." The implication is that he was immersing for the remission of sins. To this Campbell added as his final paragraph to the essay: "What might be done if this matter was generally well understood and ably proclaimed I cannot conjecture — for my own part I know of no person who has so fairly and fully tested it as he." Nothing is said in regard to Scott and his "experiment," and if Campbell is correct, then Secrest was preaching what Scott termed the ancient gospel at the time when he sat at the Mahoning Association when Scott was appointed evangelist. Campbell had visited personally with Secrest at the meeting of the Mahoning Association on August 27 and said that Secrest told him then he had immersed over three hundred in the past three months, and upon inquiry, had said that he immersed them "into the name of Jesus for remission of sins." *The Christian Baptist,* Volume V (October 1, 1827), p. 71.

16. Walter Scott, "Death of Joseph Gaston," *The Evangelist,* Volume VI (February, 1835), p. 47.

17. Hayden, p. 85.

18. Nathan J. Mitchell, *Reminiscences and Incidents in the Life and Travels of a Pioneer Preacher of the "Ancient" Gospel; With a few Characteristic Discourses* (Cincinnati: Chase and Hall, Publishers, 1877), p. 47.

19. Hayden, p. 81.

20. Errett Gates, *The Story of the Churches: The Disciples of Christ* (New York: The Baker and Taylor Co., 1905), p. 193.

21. Hayden, p. 113.

22. *Ibid,* pp. 111-112.

23. *Ibid,* pp. 112-113.

24. Gates, p. 193.

25. *Ibid,* pp. 124-125.

26. *Ibid,* pp. 427-428.

27. Winfred Garrison, editor, *The Reformation of the Nineteenth Century: A Series of Historical Sketches* (St. Louis: Christian Publishing Company, 1901), pp. 90-91.

28. Rogers, *Barton W. Stone,* pp. 71-72.

29. Mitchell, pp. 31-34.

30. *Ibid,* pp. 50-55.

31. *Ibid,* p. 58.

32. Wilcox, pp. 175-176.

33. Letter from J.D. White, Georgetown, Ohio, dated November 25, 1830. Stone, *The Christian Messenger,* Volume V (January, 1831), p. 22.

34. *Ibid,* p. 23.

35. *Ibid.*

36. John Rogers, *Autobiography of Elder Samuel Rogers* (Cincinnati: Standard Publishing Company, 1909), pp. 36-43.

37. John Rogers, "Life and Times of John Rogers," p. 75.

38. A descrepancy of dates appear here in the *Autobiography of Elder Samuel*

Rogers regarding this tour. While no exact date is placed on it in the book, it appears in sequence of events that would place it in either 1823 or 1824. Rogers stated that it was after this tour that he first heard Alexander Campbell preach in Wilmington, Ohio, in 1825. John Rogers kept a journal of this trip and records the entries in 1827, which seems to be confirmed by his visit to Campbell's home when his wife was bedridden and near death, an event which happened shortly after this visit.

39. John Rogers, p. 103.

40. *Ibid.* According to his journal he arrived at Campbell's home on August 31, 1827, and left the next day. The shortness of the stay was probably due to the ill health of Campbell's wife, for whom John prayed at her bedside before leaving. John's comment in his journal regarding this meeting was, "I had much agreeable, & I trust profitable conversation with him." For the reader's benefit, this was only eight days after the meeting of the Mahoning Baptist Association where Walter Scott received appointment.

41. *Ibid*, pp. 105-108. Samuel arrived home ahead of John, returning to Clinton County while John returned to his home in Kentucky. Samuel arrived home in late August, and made two short stops after leaving Secrest, who, according to Campbell, was at this time espousing and practicing baptism for remission of sins.

42. *Ibid*, p. 111. Rogers gives the date for this event as 1825 as previously noted. If, as he states, it came after the tour to Virginia, then it had to have been shortly afterwards. A letter appeared in the April, 1828, issue of *The Christian Baptist* from a correspondent at Antioch stating that the church had started observing weekly communion on the third Sunday in January and had been observing it steadfastly ever since. So if Campbell's sermon at Wilmington was the catalyst for this, the sermon must have been preached in the fall of 1827.

43. *Ibid*, pp. 113-114.

44. Wilcox, p. 134.

45. It is difficult to put an exact date on his acceptance and public preaching of this doctrine. When he returned from the trip through the east, having spent a limited amount of time with Campbell, a time of revival broke out in the church at Concord where he preached, reporting that for some time prior to this the church had made no advances in either numbers or holiness. People gathered, Rogers reported, "and listened with great attention and seriousness, to the exhibitions of the Gospel." In less than two months time he immersed fifty-two people. "Unusual seriousness prevades the neighborhood generally, and many are enquiring, 'What must we do to be saved?'" Recalling that Rogers visited Campbell just after the Mahoning Association meeting where Campbell had conversed with John Secrest on this matter, it is quite possible that Rogers may have carried this doctrine home with him, but not certain. The language used in his letter is characteristic of the correspondent later in *The Christian Messenger* who held to that belief, and is the reason for citing it now. See *The Christian Messenger,* Volume II (December, 1827), pp. 40-41.

46. Rogers, "Life and Times of John Rogers," p. 98.

47. Preaching tours offered opportunity for contact among the preachers. Daniel Long and J.N. Long, accompanied by Isaac N. Walter, all Christian Church preachers, traveled together for a tour of the eastern churches. They reported in their letters to Stone for publication in *The Christian Messenger* that they had visited with John Secrest at Westchester, Ohio, and E. Palmer at Smithfield, Ohio, including a report of their work. The tour began on June 7, 1827, continuing at least into the month of September. (See Volume I, p. 262 and 275 for letters from Walter and

Daniel Long.)

48. Madison Evans, *Biographical Sketches of Pioneer Preachers in Indiana* (Philadelphia: J. Challen and Sons, 1862), p. 32.

49. *Ibid,* pp. 32-33.

50. The exact time of this proposal is uncertain.

51. Barton W. Stone, "A Letter from Elder J. Hatchitt, to the Editor, dated July 25th, 1828, Ia. Bartholomew County," *The Christian Messenger,* Volume II (September, 1828), p. 260.

52. Commodore W. Cauble, *Disciples of Christ in Indiana: Achievements of a Century* (Indianapolis: Meigs Publishing Co., 1930), p. 34.

53. *Ibid,* pp. 26-29. See also Madison Evans, *Biographical Sketches of the Pioneer Preachers in Indiana* (Philadelphia: J. Challen and Sons, 1862), pp. 33-34.

54. Evans, pp. 135-136.

55. The first initial was erroneously omitted in the printing in *The Christian Messenger,* but undoubtedly was John, the Reformer preacher at Flat Rock.

56. Barton W. Stone, "Religious Intelligence," *The Christian Messenger,* Volume VI (January, 1832), pp. 28-29. Letter from Longley dated December 24, 1831.

57. Evans, p. 113.

58. Barton W. Stone, "Extract of a Letter from Elder D. Osborn, dated Franklin County, Ia. December 16, 1830," *The Christian Messenger,* Volume V (February, 1831), p. 39.

59. Belle Stanford, *Autobiography and Sermons of Elder Elijah Martindale* (Indianapolis: Carlon and Hollenbeck, Printers, 1892), p. 20.

60. *Ibid,* pp. 26-27.

61. Evans, pp. 285-286.

62. Nathaniel S. Haynes, *History of the Disciples of Christ in Illinois, 1819-1914* (Cincinnati: The Standard Publishing Company, 1915), p. 27.

63. Alonzo W. Fortune, *The Disciples in Kentucky* (The Convention of the Christian Churches in Kentucky, 1932), p. 114.

64. Barton W. Stone, *The Christian Messenger,* Volume III (October, 1829), Contains no heading, but is a report on the annual meeting.

65. Stone, *The Christian Messenger,* Volume IV (October, 1830), p. 256. A report of the annual meeting for 1830.

66. Stone, "Revivals," *The Christian Messenger,* Volume III (September, 1829), pp. 258-259.

67. Barton W. Stone, "Extract of a letter from Elder Adam Vickrey, dated Monticello, Ky. Dec. 16th, 1830," *The Christian Messenger,* Volume V (February, 1830), p. 37.

68. *Ibid.*

69. Fortune, pp. 115-116.

70. Barton W. Stone, (No heading), *The Christian Messenger,* Volume III (September, 1829), p. 261.

71. *Ibid.*

72. *Ibid, p. 262.*

73. *Ibid.*

74. Murch, *Christians Only,* pp. 110-111. The pages of the *Messenger* are rather silent regarding events "behind the scene" during this period of time.

75. Stone, "Union," *The Christian Messenger,* Volume V (August, 1831), p.

180.

76. *Ibid,* pp. 181-182.

77. I state this in regard to the Lexington and Georgetown areas. Later developments from the Christian Church segment that refused to unite in other parts of the country indicate major differences in practice as well as theory.

78. Alexander Campbell, "Reply on Union, Communion, and the Name Christian," *The Millennial Harbinger,* Volume II (September, 1831), p. 390.

79. *Ibid,* pp. 390-391.

80. *Ibid,* p. 391.

81. *Ibid,* p. 395.

82. Stone, "Remarks on A. Campbell's Reply on Union, Communion, and the Name Christian," *The Christian Messenger,* Volume V, (November, 1831), p. 248-249.

83. A. Campbell, "The Christian Messenger," *The Millennial Harbinger,* Volume II, (December 5, 1831), p. 557.

84. *Ibid.*

85. *Ibid.*

86. *Ibid,* p. 558.

87. John Rogers, *J. T. Johnson,* p. 367.

88. *Ibid.*

89. *Ibid,* p. 369.

5

UNION IN KENTUCKY

INTRODUCTION

The differences between Campbell and Stone did not deter the efforts in Kentucky to unite the two groups. Following the lead of Stone and John T. Johnson, several preachers and church members met for two separate meetings to discuss the possibility of a union. At the final meeting held in Lexington union efforts started that succeeded almost unanimously in bringing the two bodies together in Kentucky.

UNION IN CENTRAL KENTUCKY

The joint meetings for union of the Christians and Reformed Baptists happened according to plan. The

Georgetown meeting occurred December 23-26, 1831, followed by the Lexington meeting December 30, 1831, through January 2, 1832, at the Hill Street church. A large crowd gathered in Lexington for the meeting, and was heralded as "not a meeting of Elders or Preachers only, but a popular assembly — *a mass meeting* of the brethren."[1] They came to discuss points of difference and decide whether or not union could occur, and if so, upon what terms. Many thought the differences were too great and questioned its feasibility.[2]

The meeting house was filled to capacity on Saturday, New Year's Day. Several preachers attended from both sides, but the absence of many notable leaders from nearby communities could have disheartened lesser men.[3] Stone and John Smith were selected to speak with the instructions to "avoid the spirit and manner of controversy, and give their views of the plan of union freely, but without reference to party distinctions."[4] Accepting this advice, Stone and Smith withdrew to discuss the proposal. Stone asked, "What is your choice, my brother? Will you speak first or last?" Smith said his mind was made up what he would say and it mattered little to him when he spoke, so Stone asked him to speak first.[5] Opening this historical meeting Smith said,

> God has but one people on the earth. He has given to them but one Book, and therein exhorts and commands them to be one family. A union, such as we plead for — a union of God's people on that one Book — must, then, be practicable.
>
> Every Christian desires to stand complete in the whole will of God. The prayer of the Savior, and the whole tenor of his teaching, clearly show that it is God's will that his children should be united. To the Christian, then, such a union must be desirable.[6]

Jesus, said Smith, did not pray for an amalgamation of sects, but for union upon divine principles founded upon the Bible. Controversial theological questions had been argued for centuries, he said, and still remained unsettled. He proposed the only answer rested in using the language of the Scriptures without speculating on various theories.

> While there is but one faith, there may be ten thousand opinions; and hence, if Christians are ever to be one, they must be one in faith, and not in opinion. When certain subjects arise, even in conversation or social discussion, about which there is a contrariety of opinion and sensitiveness of feeling, speak of them in the words of the Scriptures, and no offense will be given, and no pride of doctrine will be encouraged. We may even come, in the end, by thus speaking the same things, to think the same things.
>
> For several years past, I have stood pledged to meet the religious world, or any part of it, on the ancient Gospel and order of things, as presented in the words of the Book. This is the foundation on which Christians once stood, and on it they can, and ought to, stand again. From this I can not depart to meet any man, or set of men, in the wide world. While, for the sake of peace and Christian union, I have long since waived the public maintenance of any speculation I may hold, *yet not one Gospel fact, commandment, or promise, will I surrender for the world!*
>
> Let us, then, my brethren, be no longer Campbellites or Stoneites, or New Lights or Old Lights, or any other kind of lights, but let us all come to the Bible, and to the Bible alone, as the only book in the world that can give us all the Light we need.[7]

Stone then followed, speaking on some of the same issues and assuring the audience that he fully agreed that controversial issues, unsettled through the centuries, should never find a place in the pulpit. He then said, "I have not one objection to the ground laid down by him as the true scriptural basis of union among the people of God; and I am willing to give him, now and here, my hand."[8] As he spoke, he turned and "offered to Smith a hand trembling with rapture and brotherly love, and it was grasped by a hand full of honest pledges of fellowship, and the union was virtually accomplished."[9]

> It was now proposed that all who felt willing to unite on these principles should express that willingness by giving one another the hand of fellowship; and elders and teachers hastened forward, and joined

their hands and hearts in joyful accord. A song arose, and brethren and sisters, with many tearful greetings, ratified and confirmed the union. On Lord's day, they broke the loaf together, and in that sweet and solemn communion, again pledged to each other their brotherly love.[10]

Williams overstated the situation as the union was far from consummation. It required much more than a few handshakes and an emotional reaction from the audience gathered. This only marked the beginning of a long, difficult task of creating union over the entire state of Kentucky.

Various preachers and elders attended, but did not come as delegates. They returned to their churches, presented the propositions of the union to them, and encouraged cooperation by uniting. But many of the congregations had no representation and in order to inform and attempt to unite them, measures formerly agreed upon by the leaders were adopted. John Smith, a Reformer, and John Rogers, a Christian, agreed to serve as evangelists to travel among the churches to foster union and to convince all of the sincerity of the union.[11] John T. Johnson agreed to serve as co-editor with Stone of *The Christian Messenger*,[12] and to serve as treasurer to receive and disburse funds sent by the churches to support the evangelists. Establishing the machinery to effect the union throughout the state set this venture apart from the previous local unions elsewhere. They purposed this would be state-wide, and hopefully multi-state wide.

Johnson, in his first editorial in the *Messenger* said,

I pledge the exertion of my humble powers in cleaning away the cobwebs of speculation — in suppressing conjecture — in discarding from religion all the traditions and philosophies of men — and in enforcing the indispensible necessity of an immediate return to the word of God.[13]

He recognized such an undertaking would be difficult.

> We are well aware, we have to encounter, in this noblest and best of all enterprises, the deep rooted prejudices of many of the pious, as well as the rancorous opposition of worldly minded professors; . . .[14]

He appealed to all who had united on "the King's highway" to live a life full of mercy and good fruits while presenting the truth in boldness. Then, sounding much like the leading Reformer of Bethany, he wrote,

> Let it be graven on every Christian's mind, that he who does most to unite the followers of Jesus, favors most the conversion of the world — and he who does most in opposition to such union, does most in opposition to the will of the King, and against the conversion of the world.[15]

Johnson was convinced that this union was an absolute essential. Stone, later writing about the union, said,

> Johnson testified, "What could we do but unite? We both compared notes. We found ourselves congregated on the same divine creed, the Bible. We had the same King — the same faith — the same law. We, reciprocally, had discarded all human speculations and opinions, as foreign to the gospel, and unworthy of the serious attention of Christians. The name under which we rallied was the same. We could not do otherwise than unite in Christian love, fellowship and effort in the glorious work of reform."[16]

The editors announced the union in simple style; "We are happy to announce to our brethren, and to the world, the union of Christians in fact in our country." They reported the meetings and arrangements, stating they had never witnessed "more love, union, and harmony, than was manifested at these meetings. Since the last meeting we have heard of the good effects. The union is spreading like fire in dry stubble." From the information gathered at this point the churches were "highly pleased, and . . . determined to co-operate in the work."[17]

George W. Elley, a Reformer preacher in the area of

Nicholasville, Kentucky, immediately wrote to Walter Scott, editor of *The Evangelist*, informing him of the union. He wrote,

> Permit me to inform you of a mighty conquest which truth and the love of it, have lately obtained in Lexington, Ky. at a three days' meeting . . . by Brethren John Smith, John T. Johnson, B.W. Stone, Rogers T. Smith, J. Creath, sen.[18] and others, in the Christian Brethren *Meeting-House;* when all seemed to be inspired with a wish to promote the good cause of Gospel truth: Brothers John Smith and Barton W. Stone, the first formerly a Calvanistic (sic) Baptist, the other, one of those denominated a Christian, arose on Saturday to address the people, when they both declared that they had no doubt speculated much for the last ten or twenty years in relation to Gospel truth, as well upon the subject of the trinity, as upon other subjects, that they were not conscious of having effected any good by it, but some evil. That for the future, they now both determined to cease from all speculation upon the oracles of God; stop where they stopped; and go when they commanded; and in a word, to oppose every thing else as the standard of Divine truth.[19]

Elley viewed the union as a great triumph, not only because plans for a greater union were constructed, but both sides had admitted they had previously strayed in several speculations and would now give up these tendencies to rest their case on the Bible. He concluded,

> When we see, Bro. Scott, old men who have been the leaders of a sect for years, cast their crown at the feet of Jesus and submit alone to him, we are bound to believe that it proceeds from the love of the truth, and not the aggrandizement of a party. Old Bro. Stone is a man of talent and much reputation for piety, and I rejoice at the prospects of seeing before long the mighty army which will be marshalled in the field upon these glorious principles. It is proposed to employ Brothers John Smith and Rogers, to labour for the next twelve months amongst the churches in order to promote this wished for union, and to convert the aliens.[20]

CAMPBELL'S COMMENTS ON THE UNION

Historians have viewed Campbell's response to the union

differently, interpreting it from "shock"[21] to simply seeing it as premature.[22] Campbell's biographer, a contemporary of Campbell, wrote that Campbell viewed it as premature. This position makes sense when it is understood that in Ohio prior to 1832, many of the Christians simply joined the Reformers, fully accepting the views of Campbell. An unknown source of information informed Campbell in 1830 that

> Many of the Christian preachers have come out for immersion for the remission of sins. I was informed the other day, that in the commonwealth of Ohio, alone, there were 72 of those called Christian preachers who proclaim immersion for remission, and only 11 who oppose it.[23]

With such reports in hand and knowledge of past events in Ohio, it is possible that Campbell's attitude toward the union came more out of loss of hope that what happened in Ohio would happen elsewhere. If this is true, then he would have seen it as premature.

Interpreting Campbell's response as shocked seems somewhat harsh. True, Campbell and Stone had discussed vital issues of differences and still stood apart in some areas. Campbell viewed the Christians as simply being anti-creedal, anti-trinitarian, anti-council, and anti-sectarian who had not traveled the full road of reform. But he had been laboring for twenty years for Christian unity and some recognition should be given this factor.

Campbell did close the last issue of the *Millennial Harbinger* in 1831, as West cites, "on a sour note." However, this was not the last issue of the paper before he learned of the union. The first edition in 1832 carries a date mark of January 2, the same date that the union meetings were coming to completion in Kentucky. He obviously sent this edition to the press without knowledge of the union. The issue does, however, carry a news item about the harmonious attitude that prevailed between the two bodies at Georgetown. In summarizing the report Campbell wrote,

> We rejoice to hear that the utmost harmony and christian love
> prevail, not only amongst the disciples composing this congregation,
> but between them and the disciples meeting under the *Christian*
> name in connexion with brother Stone in Georgetown,
> notwithstanding the sparring between us editors. . . .
>
> How the Lord's cause would prosper in this happy land, if all who
> speak to men on religion were governed by such a sentiment and feel-
> ing as the following. It is from a letter written to me from our very in-
> telligent and pious brother Johnson: — "Indeed, brother Campbell, I
> care not what the world may say of me. I am for my Saviour's
> religion. To practise and teach it in its purity is my greatest earthly
> delight. I go forth not calculating the consequences to myself, fully
> persuaded that so certainly as Jesus reigns King of kings and Lord of
> lords, his truth is mighty and will prevail." Should this sentiment kin-
> dle a similar ardor in any breast, I am aware this brother will par-
> don me for quoting from a private letter without his consent.[24]

Campbell was not totally ignorant of the sentiments between
the two bodies in Kentucky, especially in the Georgetown
area. Having commended them for the spirit of union in that
area, it seems improbable that his rejoicing over a local situation would turn to dismay when he learned these same men
were attempting to bring union throughout the state.

The same issue of the *Harbinger* contained an article
based on a letter from John Brice of Georgetown to a person
in Fredricksburg, Virginia, which obviously fell into Campbell's hands, telling about the two groups uniting at
Georgetown, calling them Arians and Campbellites.[25] The
writer of the letter believed both groups were heretical and
Campbell addressed the letter. He said that if the two groups
had united, it rested on the principle that neither Campbell
nor Arius was the bond of union or masters of their faith.
Since the author of the letter did not state it, wrote Campbell,
he did not know which of the two was the worst ingredient
in the union, the Campbellites or the Arians, but since the
author believed both groups were heretical, one joining the

other would not purify either. But, reasoned Campbell, had either group joined the Calvinistic Baptists, then Brice would approve the arrangement, since then the "heretical ingredient would have been neutralized by the purifying influence of super-oxygenated Calvinism."[26] He then developed the difference between uniting with a party and joining a party.

> If a Papist should unite with a Protestant, or a Protestant with a Papist, the compound would be the same, provided the parties met on the compromise of half their principles; but if the Catholic compromised nothing; and the Protestant all, the compound would be pure Popery; or if the Protestant compromised nothing, and the Catholic all, the compound would be pure Protestantism.[27]

From this logic he made his point; the Campbellites had not joined the Arians,

> . . . for I can vouch for the fact, that in the case alluded to, those stigmatized "Campbellites" have surrendered nothing, not a single truth that they either believed or taught; and they who have united with us from all parties have met us upon the ancient gospel and the ancient order of things.[28]

Neither did Campbell say that the Arians had joined the Campbellites, but united. Both parties, therefore, by illustration, met upon the "ancient gospel and ancient order of things."

A clear understanding of Campbell's position regarding the union can be seen from a second illustration; "lines drawn from the circumference of any circle towards its centre, will meet in the same point."[29] This central point was the ancient gospel and the ancient order of things. He believed he and his followers had moved from former positions to the middle of the circle, waiting for others to come to that same point. The logical conclusion is that Campbell looked upon his group as formerly giving up their speculations while others were still in the process.

As insignificant as this might seem, it is important in order to understand Campbell's comments on the proposed state-wide union. He announced the union in his paper in the March, 1832, edition by quoting from *The Christian Messenger*.[30] He mentioned that numerous letters had been received from Kentucky regarding the union events at Lexington. Without question one of the correspondents was Elley, who had written to Walter Scott and undoubtedly also to Campbell.[31]

Campbell's comments focused upon the evangelists, Smith and Rogers, and their proposed labors. He bid them Godspeed in their efforts. Instead, however, of terming John Smith as formerly a "Reformer" and Rogers formerly a "Christian," as the editors of the *Messenger* identified them, he referred to Smith as formerly a "Baptist." This terminology kept him consistent with his logic of the circle illustration and the distinction between uniting and joining. Had he labeled Smith a "Reformer," he would have been forced to say the Christians joined the Reformers or that the Reformers compromised their position. Using the term "Baptist" permitted him to view both as leaving their former speculations and coming to the center of the circle. Elley, in his correspondence to Scott, had termed Smith "formerly a Calvinistic Baptist,"[32] performing a great favor for Campbell.

The next logical stroke for Campbell was enunciating the former positions of the men to show they had left their former designations and had accepted his reformation. They had both moved to the center of the circle. He wrote,

> The sublimities of trinitarian calvinism and the sublimities of unitarian arminianism adorned their speeches and animated their strains. But now they have each renounced *own-ism,* and have protested against all human *isms,* (their own amongst the number;) and now they plead *the ancient order of things;* an item of which, and *but an item of which,* is *the ancient gospel.* They are now to make converts to God and the Lamb, and to persuade those called Baptist, those called Christians, and all other sects, christian and infidel, that they must

reform and *do works worthy of reformation.* They now go forth to plead for the long-lost honors of the Holy Twelve — to bring the disciples to keep *all the commandments* of the Lord and Saviour — to keep the ordinances as delivered by the Apostles.[33]

These men occupied the very position which Campbell hoped to see in all men; they had come fully into his reform. Therefore he could give his blessing to their work without any reservations, even though he may have thought the union premature, hoping others from the Christians would come to the center of the circle. He added;

In such an undertaking, who that loves the saviour, would not bid them God speed? It is not, then, to preach the necessity of *union* amongst *professors,* nor to *baptize persons* and let them fall into the desolating order of things which has so long obtained in the sects to which they formerly belonged: — it is to bring *the christians indeed to do the things* the Lord has commanded. These brethren will say each for himself, "let my tongue cleave to the roof of my mouth, and my right hand forget its art," sooner than either are employed in preaching any thing but *the faith* once delivered to the saints, in substituting half-way expedients, professions for obedience, or in advocating any other union than a union in truth and with truth.[34]

Campbell's closing comments were, "I say, then, from the present aspect of things, we have reason to thank God and take courage, and to bid these brethren God speed."[35]

The leaders in Kentucky were moving ahead with plans without waiting to hear what Campbell had to say. John Allen Gano, one of the Reformers who participated in the work of union, wrote,

The people of God now united together in one family by thousands. Life and love prevailed through the churches at the earnest request of the churches and their elders in several of the counties around.[36]

TEMPORARY PROBLEMS AT LEXINGTON

In Lexington, after several committee meetings, the two

groups agreed to unite. The agreement was solemnized by shaking hands, singing an appropriate hymn, and agreeing to meet together February 26 for final consummation, enrolling their names together. On the previous Sunday, however, an "unfortunate blow-up" occurred. Some of the Christian brethren were unwilling to enter into the union; the point of controversy involving choice of an elder. The two groups met on February 25 and dissolved their pledge to unite. A correspondent to Campbell wrote,

> It is the *Clergy* — The *hireling system* — the *called and sent* — the *rulers* — that keep us apart. No we cannot unite under present *existing circumstances.* The present existing circumstance is this: there is not a member in either society at present whom we could appoint Elder, according to divine direction; and some of the Christian friends wished to know if they could not hire one from a sister church, with her consent, to administer the ordinances? For they believe that no person but a *preacher* has a right to administer the ordinances — such as *the breaking of the loaf* &c. and become very much alarmed at the idea of us common folks receiving the name of kings and priests to the Lord; or, as it is in the common version, according to Griesbach's standard Greek text, by Nathan Hall, "A kingdom of priests to God." Yes, sir, it is this hireling system, this divine call and mission, which forbade our union; because our union forbids this state of things. This clerical authority, this thing of Elder here, and there, and yonder, at the same time, is what caused our blow up.[37]

Campbell's comments on the rupture filled the first three pages of the next issue of his paper. He sharply criticized a bishop over more than one church, monthly or quarterly communion, clerical attention to the ordinances, and the sectarian spirit that keeps Christians separated. In concluding the article he presented again his plan for unity.

> If the christians in all sects could be drawn together, then would the only real, desirable, and permanent union, worthy of the name for the union of christians, be achieved. How to effect this has long been a question with us and many others. To us, it appears, the only practicable way to accomplish this desirable object, is to propound the

ancient gospel and the ancient order of things in the words and sentences found in the apostolic writings — to abandon all traditions and usages not found in the Record, and to make no human terms of communion.[38]

The two bodies in Lexington did not unite until July, 1835, as a result of the untiring efforts of Thomas M. Allen, minister of the Christian Church in Lexington.[39] B.F. Hall verified the union in a letter to Campbell in October, 1835; "The difficulties between the two parties are settled *finally.*"[40]

THE EARLY WORK OF SMITH AND ROGERS

Differences at Lexington did not hinder Smith and Rogers in their efforts. The work was demanding, yet they continued in the field; Rogers for three years and Smith even longer.

Smith returned to Mount Sterling after the union meetings to discover the news had preceded him. Within the hour of his arrival the elders of the congregation came to his house concerned about the rumors and reports. Unacquainted with Stone, but fully acquainted with the prejudices against him and the Christians, they believed Smith had made "a great blunder." He resolved to preach no more until he reconciled them to the union and requested the church to gather "to consider his action, and to determine, in the light of the Scriptures alone, whether he had done right or wrong."[41] When the congregation assembled Smith spoke at length, then submitted himself to their questioning. He then left them to make their decision.

The question was submitted, "Has Brother Smith done right in affiliating with the new Light party?" Such had been the force of his reasoning, and such was the influence of his character, that, after due reflection, their prejudice gave way; they were persuaded, or convinced, and their confidence in him revived. They not only acquitted him of censure, but for the most part, went cordially with him into the union.[42]

Successfully withstanding the test at Mount Sterling, he went to the other three churches he served; Somerset, Sharpsburg, and Owingsville, where the same walls of opposition and doubt prevailed. He again overcame the opposition and brought them into the union,[43] and then began on his travels to unite the two groups elsewhere.

John Rogers ministered to one of the largest congregations of the "Christians" in Kentucky, at Carlisle. There is no record of any problems with his congregations[44] over the union. From the time of Campbell's visit to Carlisle, Rogers gradually moved toward the Reformers' views and the congregations undoubtedly developed similarly, leaving him without the prejudices to overcome that Smith had. Rogers later wrote:

> It is only stating what the facts in the case require, when I say that our people were much sooner prepared for the union than the friends of A. Campbell. This is by no means strange. We had, as a people, been standing on the word of God alone for almost thirty years. We had no party name, nor party platform to support — to stand between us and union with any of God's people on the true scriptural plan of union, and his able plea for it, our people all over Kentucky, and very many in other states, most cordially embraced it, and were ready to act upon it.[45]

The reason Smith had his problems can be understood by the rest of Rogers' statement.

> On the other side, however, there were much shyness and tardiness. They believed that we ought to be one; but then it was a question whether the set time was come. There was a feeling repugnant to union with those toward whom they had so recently cherished the feelings of the most bitter hostility, as the most terrible heretics, rejecting and denying, as they had thought, almost everything that was sacred in religion![46]

Rogers, unhindered by problems in his own churches, began working among the churches before Smith. During March he went into northern Kentucky, accompanied by Joshua Irvin, and on the first Saturday evening and Sunday of the month, was at North Middleton. Rogers decided to start with the easier situations where union would be successful. When they arrived at North Middleton, they found the two congregations agreeable to union and they entered "heartily into the spirit of *this union upon the one foundation*. . . ."[47]

During the rest of March he traveled into Fleming and Mason counties, telling the churches that they had rested on the theory of union previously, now they must put it into action. He preached at Poplar Ridge, Elizaville, Bethel, Flemingsburg, Union, Wilson's Run, Beech Woods, and Mayslick. Rogers reported through the *Messenger,* ". . . I am happy to say that desire to know and do their Master's will, seems to predominate in those churches."[48]

When he returned he spent a week with Johnson,[49] probably at the Dry Run church as Rogers included it in his itinerary report and stated that Johnson accompanied him.[50] Johnson had started preaching near the old Dry Run meetinghouse in June, 1831, unable to occupy the house as it "was shut against him." In a few months he had a large crowd attending and constituted the church. The editor of the *Harbinger,* in a footnote to this report, stated, "There were three or four members of the Christian body in the neighborhood of Dry Run at the time brother Johnson commenced speaking there, who cordially received him. . . ."[51] Thus the two bodies were already working together in this community. Rogers went to preach a protracted meeting and build additional good will.

Smith sent appointments in early March to the Stockton Valley area. The tour, lasting from late March until April 20, included Somerset, Monticello, and various other places and was primarily evangelistic as no churches of either group existed in the valley.[52]

During the first two weeks of May, the two evangelists traveled together through the five-county area of Harrison, Scott, Woodford, Jessamine, and Bourbon.[53] This tour was for unification and evangelism. At Clear Creek, Rogers met and worked with the Creaths, Luke, Elley, and other Reformer preachers who were "almost, or entirely strangers" to him.[54] Smith was unable to accompany Rogers to Cane Ridge, but J.T. Johnson and other Reformer preachers were there with F.R. Palmer, the regular preacher at Cane Ridge. This meeting is significant because the teaching of baptism for remission of sins had created some stir in the churches, although most of the preachers in Kentucky had accepted it. This doctrine had never been presented from the pulpit at Cane Ridge. Rogers later wrote of this meeting:

> I shall never forget that on Monday of that meeting, for the first time at that place, I presented the teaching of Peter on the question of baptism for remission sins. I consulted brother Palmer, my senior, and a very prudent and sensible man, as to the propriety of my preaching on that subject. He consented, I thought, somewhat reluctantly: having some fears as to the result. But the results were favorable, and he was much pleased.[55]

Smith and Rogers traveled north together the last two weeks of May, once more, to Mason and Fleming counties. They were joined in some places by Aylett Raines, Walter Scott, D.S. Burnet, and others. Rogers, in his report to the *Messenger,* said nothing about unity only reporting the number of additions to the churches. Fortunately, because of an incident which Rogers thought humorous, a brief account of the meeting at Mayslick is described in his journal. At this meeting Rogers was seated between Scott and Raines, both former Reformers from the Western Reserve in Ohio, while D.S. Burnet preached. As he spoke on union Scott casually leaned across Rogers and stated to Raines, "He wishes to unite us Christians and you Campbellites.''[56] They returned back to central Kentucky from this trip going together to Dry Run, Republican, and Carlisle.[57]

> The meeting at Republican, near Lexington, about the first of June, was one of special interest. Many christians and disciples, no longer wearing these names distinctively, and caring no longer for differences of opinion, came together from all the surrounding counties, not so much to strengthen, as to enjoy their happy union. It was indeed a season of intense spiritual and social delight. Five hundred brethren and sisters, heretofore suspicious, or estranged, broke the loaf together; every eye was suffused with rapture, and ever heart glowed with brotherly love.[58]

Thomas Smith, reporting the meeting to the *Messenger* wrote, "The beneficial effects of the union, at this meeting, were much enjoyed and realised."[59] This is the first recorded instance of several churches uniting for a meeting since the Lexington gathering in January. It provided encouragement to the union.

F.W. Elley, one of the Reformer preachers who had accompanied Smith and Rogers during the first part of May, wrote a report of the activities in central Kentucky for publication in *The Evangelist*. He referred to the meeting at Republican, estimating that nearly five hundred communicants participated in breaking the loaf on Sunday and told of other places where reform was progressing. He wrote,

> Much good feeling seems to prevail between the christian and Reforming brethren, and with one heart and one soul, being animated by the same spirit, they proclaim the word of the Lord with much effect.[60]

The first union meeting in Montgomery County, a four-day meeting at Spencer meeting-house began on Friday, June 25, with the two evangelists and several other preachers present. It, too, was successful and after it ended, Rogers and

Raines went to Sharpsburg, one of Smith's congregations, showing that Smith had successfully removed their doubts about the "Christians" in permitting Rogers to come. Where doubt had previously prevailed, harmony and good will replaced it.[61]

The four-day meeting was frequently used, either for unity purposes or evangelistic intentions. During the first part of July Rogers scheduled a meeting at Carlisle where Smith preached.[62] The primary purpose of this meeting was evangelistic, but it afforded the Carlisle church an opportunity to get acquainted with the other evangelist.

August found the two men working sometimes together, sometimes separate; into Nicholas, Fleming, and Clark counties.[63] The biggest event of the month was the first annual meeting of the Reformers in the old North District. This meeting, appointed a year previously at Somerset after the association was dissolved, was held in Bath County at Sharpsburg meeting-house on August 17 as an experiment. Preachers from both groups attended and Johnson wrote,

> We were captivated with the love which reigned among the brethren, and the zeal which was manifested for the conversion of sinners. Oh! that love and union may abound everywhere as at Sharpsburg! . . .
> On Lord's day we partook, with several hundred, as near as we can guess, of the Lord's Supper. It was a most interesting scene. If sectarian leaders who busy themselves in misrepresenting us — in charging us with impure motives so far as a union of christians has been effected — and who, according to their wishes, are perpetually crying out that the union can not last — had been present, they might have been convinced of the benefits growing out of one.[64]

The evangelists continued their labors until the middle of October. Smith wrote, "I am constantly going, and am much encouraged. Prospects are flattering in every place where I have been."[65] Most of their travels were in central Kentucky. Rogers returned to northern Kentucky during the last part of

September and the first part of October and crossed the river to Georgetown, Ohio.[66]

OPPOSITION TO THE UNION

The evangelists were not without opposition in their labors. Rogers later wrote:

> It was not to be expected, that a Union between two large bodies of people, entertaining speculations so antagonistic as ours had been, could at once unite with out opposition from individuals on both sides. Hence Bro: Smith, my fellow-Evangelist, was called to account, like Peter, for going in among our people & communing with them. It was charged in doing so, he was trampling upon the great principles of Union as taught by A. Campbell. So, some of our people opposed the Union, as a violation of the principles of reformation, as, at first set forth by Stone & his Co-laborers.[67]

Smith, having to answer all the doubts of the Reformers, found several prejudices confronting him, the greatest being the attitude toward Stone by many of the Reformers, "a formidable barrier to union." Some, demanding a "Thus saith the Lord" for every action, questioned the idea of the group at Lexington selecting Rogers and Smith as evangelists and pledging to pay them for their services. These refused to cooperate in supporting the evangelists and discouraged others from helping.[68]

Smith, in answer to these objections by the Reformers, wrote and published an article in the *Messenger* for the benefit of the Reformers. He attempted to answer their objections and present a true portrait of the "Christians" to his readers. He wrote,

> When we fell in company with the Christian teachers, we conversed freely and friendly together. With some one or other of them we have conversed on all the supposed points of difference between them and

123

the Reformers, and all the erroneous sentiments which I had heard laid to their charge, such as the following: . . .[69]

He listed and answered the following objections: (1) they deny the atonement; (2) they receive the unimmersed into the church and have communion with them; (3) they are unitarians; and (4) the Reformers, in communing with them, "sanction all the sectarian speculations of all those who are called by name throughout the United States." He concluded with a short statement about the name "Christian," and an exhortation to his brethren asking them to show him where he had acted contrary to the Bible in his actions.[70] When Rogers read the article, he wrote that it contained

> . . . a fair and clear statement, as far as it goes, of the principles and practices of the Christian brethren in these regions, and not only here, but generally in the West. I do, therefore, confidently hope that it will be greatly useful in promoting the good work of union and co-operation among those who have acknowledged and submitted to the one Lord. . . .[71]

Not all of the opposition centered on doctrine. Rumors spread about the amount of money the evangelists were receiving and the figure went as high as $75.00 per month. This was intended to hurt their influence among the churches.[72] Rogers thought the opposition came because of fears about the union. He wrote later,

> The writer can never forget that, though generally received with great cordiality where he went on the mission of union, he was treated on a few occasions, some six months after the union had taken place, with marked indifference and neglect. The fears, however, which superinduced such treatment, were soon removed, and all was kindness and good feeling.[73]

He did not mean that all went smoothly after this. He later wrote that "it required great prudence, & kindness, &

forbearance in our movements to keep the congregation together, & prevent schism and strife."[74]

They also encountered opposition outside the two bodies. When people from other groups would talk to the Christians they would say,

> We thought well of you: you are a praying, spiritual people, who believe in experimental religion, but you have united with these Christless Campbellites, who deny all heart religion — who believe in water salvation — water regeneration; & much more to the same effect.[75]

Then when they would talk with the Reformers they would remark, "We deeply regret your union with these Stoneites; why, they deny the Trinity, the Divinity of Christ, the efficacy of his blood, and much more of like import."[76] Rumors were kindled also to destroy the influence of the evangelists. In one community where outside opposition was strong, Smith had a friend approach him and say, "We did not expect to see you, Brother Smith, for we heard a few days ago, that you had been prosecuted in Mount Sterling, for stealing forty hogs, and had been put in jail."[77]

PROGRESS OF THE UNION

Opposition did not restrain the rapid progress of the work. Aided by others besides the two evangelists, in Pendleton County some from both groups met together on June 19-20, 1832, at William Cleaveland's to unite. After the communion service, John W. Roberts said the two bodies had so much in common they ought to be one, calling on all who would unite together to come forward and enroll their names. "They all flowed together with the best feeling; a union of all present took place."[78] Roberts' word choice for what occurred; they "flowed together;" is excellent terminology to describe the effecting of the union in Kentucky. John Allen Gano used the same terminology to describe it in his memorial sermon to Barton W. Stone at Cane Ridge on June 22, 1845.[79]

At Wadesboro, Kentucky, the two bodies united in that county anticipating "that great good will result."[80] In August, "the disciples in Covington" had a two-day meeting with Stone, the chief speaker, accompanied by Scott, James Challen, Andrews, and Ellis, indicating that this congregation embraced the union.[81] It also indicates that the editors of the *Messenger,* Stone and Johnson, were active in traveling to promote union, as well as writing to create a good will and erase barriers.

Many looked forward to the annual meeting in October, 1832, at the Clintonville church in Bourbon County, expecting a report on union. At the meeting

> John Smith and John Rogers now rehearsed their travels, and cheered the friends of union and reform by their account of the remarkable success of the truth during the past few months. From their general report then given, it appears that several hundred persons in the few surrounding counties had, within that short time, been immersed into Christ, and that the two parties, in nearly every place which they had visited, had affiliated in work and worship as one people.[82]

Optimism prevailed. Johnson wrote in October that the work of union

> . . . is accomplishing much faster than we anticipated. . . . Thus far, we have every reason for joy and rejoicing. This year has developed more fully and powerful effects of a practical union of Christians; and the result bids us be steadfast, immovable; and to march on, always abounding in the work of the Lord.[83]

In the next issue he stated that the work had succeeded beyond his "most sanguine anticipations."[84]

The union also generated evangelism. A correspondent

wrote to Campbell, "The reform, I suppose, has received an addition of five, this year, to every one of all the other sects."[85] While some problems still existed, the Kentucky brethren were quite optimistic about their union. Stone and Johnson admitted the subject of baptism still had not been wholly settled by the end of the first year, but they would not let this difference destroy or hinder the union. "We still design," they wrote, "to collect and unite the scattered flock . . ."[86]

The two evangelists were placed upon the field to continue their labors in 1833 and 1834, but in 1835 Rogers, due to his wife's health, had to withdraw.[87] During these three years they were workhorses for the union. Both men looked back upon this period of time as the greatest years of their lives.[88] Rogers, looking back some twenty years later, said that "perhaps, all things considered, no three years of our history were ever more successful than the years 1832-3-4."[89]

Most of Rogers' and Smith's travels during 1833 and 1834, according to their reports, were primarily evangelistic, but also "promoting and confirming the union of the two people."[90] During the summer of 1833, cholera broke out in Kentucky and hindered the evangelists from traveling. Fear of the dreaded disease affected many people, resulting in large numbers of converts. Between the cordial effects of the union and the cholera, 1833 was a more successful year than any previous.[91]

Several places still existed, after the first year, where union had not yet been completed. The church at Paris favored the union from the very beginning, but the two bodies did not unite until 1834; the problem centering in division in the Baptist church. The Baptists attempted to dismiss the preacher, Gates, and failed by a vote of nearly three to one, leading to separation of the minority group. The Christian Church had embraced the ideas of the Reformation and James Challen led them into union in August, 1834. He preached at the Reformed Baptist Church on John 17 on the third Lord's Day in August and the congregation adopted the resolution:

> Whereas, owing to the confused and disorganized condition in which this church finds itself, growing out of the unfortunate division which took place in the body some time since and to which other causes have also contributed; and there being some things in its constitution which we do not approve — *Therefore resolved,* That we will enrol ourselves anew; and all who have been baptized (i.e. immersed) upon a profession of their faith in the Lord Jesus, and are in good standing, and walking orderly as followers of our common Lord, are affectionately invited to come forward and enrol their names also; and those who thus enrol themselves shall be considered a church of our Lord Jesus Christ, "built upon the foundation of the apostles and prophets, Jesus Christ himself being the chief corner stone, to be called the Church of Christ in Paris, and we will then go into an organization of the body after the model of the apostolic churches."[92]

Nearly all those present who belonged to the two bodies came forward and enrolled their names. Others followed later and on the last Sunday of the month, met together and started a three-day meeting.[93]

The transition did not come easy for most churches. Paris, Leesburg, and Mount Carmel all embraced the union but had not fully accepted Campbell's notions. One of the pioneer preachers recorded in his notebook,

> These churches were now prospering and in peace although they had not as yet any of them practically attained to that order which in theory nearly all agreed in private chats was Scriptural and desirable. So hard is it to reform in the order; religious societies not organized according to the word of the Lord at their birth.[94]

In northern Kentucky two churches of the "Christians" entered the union much to the dismay of their organizer, Matthew Gardner. The Dry Creek church, about seven miles south of Covington, was organized by Gardner in either 1827 or 1828 at the request of John Ellis, who became the preacher when Gardner left. In the words of Gardner, "Campbellism came along under the Christian name, and the church and preacher were carried away together by their dissimulations."[95]

The other church was located about five miles northwest of Maysville. After Gardner organized the church Elder Roberts from Licken Knobs came to preach for them, having sentiments toward the Reformers, and successfully gained some followers in the congregation. But his character did not match his preaching; he borrowed money from different individuals and would not repay it; and the church broke up because of him. Three different factions evolved from the division; some went to the Methodists, some stood apart from any group and "some went into Campbellism," and continued in the stone meeting-house.[96]

Union efforts failed along the Big Sandy River in Eastern Kentucky. Abraham Snethen was the first "Christian" preacher to travel into the Big Sandy area, preaching all along the river before returning to his Ohio home.[97] He did not support the union and may be the reason for opposition from the churches. John Smith traveled into the Big Sandy area[98] but with no success. J.J. Summerbell's short resume of the American Christian Conference in 1886 listed only two conferences in Kentucky; the Big Sandy Conference, which had not reported its number of churches at the time of publication, and the Kentucky Conference, which covered the northeastern section of the state and listed twenty-four churches.[99] From the language of the Christian preachers on the Ohio side of the river who did not go along with the union, it appears that the majority of these churches were organized later. The union was almost unanimous in Kentucky, but some Christian churches did stay out of it.

Matthew Gardner, a Christian preacher in Ohio and a formidable opponent to the union, maintained that the union in Kentucky was not as successful as advertised. He admitted most of the Christian preachers in Kentucky, in his terminology, had "gone over to Mr. C's reform," only those who had feared opposing Campbell's doctrines "lest they are overpowered and put down." He stated that most of the churches in Kentucky, if possible, would like to have preachers on the original ground which the old Christians maintained.[100]

In 1841, nine years after the first union meeting, a letter appeared in the *Christian Palladium,* a publication of the group in the state of New York, from a Kentucky Christian. He wrote,

> The Christians in this section of Kentucky, were once very numerous, until Mr. Campbell came in with his disorganizing theory, which divided and well nigh destroyed the church. The Christians, before embracing this doctrine, enjoyed religion, attended the house of worship, and you might hear their shouts of praise, and praying for more heart felt religion. The work went on about right; but these members who have since imbraced this negative system have become so lukewarm and lifeless, that you may meet them in the court yard, and cannot tell them from sinners by their fruits; their worship is nothing but a form. And these members who once could shout and praise God, now tell them about justification by faith, and *experimental religion,* and they will laugh you to scorn.
> . . . However there is a little few who yet stand on the old ground of Christian liberty in Ky., and have a desire to see the work go on.[101]

Obviously, very little of the old Christian churches still remained a few years after the union.

Numerous points of issue existed between the two groups that had to be settled before the union was completed. The biggest difficulty centered about remission of sins in baptism. Since this was a bigger issue in Ohio where debates ensued, the main discussion will be deferred until later. The manner in which some of the more adamant preachers handled the subject created the greatest problems. Williams wrote,

> Concerning the doctrine of *baptism for the remission of sins,* it is proper to say, that while very generally received by the Christians at

the time of the union, it had been perverted by imprudent teachers to the injury of the cause; so that some did not accept it, or held it in a sense different from that in which it was generally propounded.[102]

Rogers, attempting to soften the untactful approach of some of the preachers, wrote an article in the *Messenger* asking for a Christian spirit on both sides.

Some among us have embraced it cordially; others reject it. What then: Shall those who embrace it, condemn those, who tho' they believe in immersion, cannot go the whole length with us in this matter? God forbid. Or shall those who do not receive it, condemn those who do? I trust not. Charity forbids it. Our principles forbid it. Here then, dear brethren, firmly united upon the book, upon the highest ground that can be taken, let us move forward, investigating every religious subject testing every sentiment by our Creed; cultivating the love of truth & holiness; never making any opinion a test of Christian fellowship; never resting till we are filled with the knowledge of His will . . .''[103]

The next year, 1833, Rogers asked teachers who encountered those who did not agree with their doctrine to deal with them with Christian feeling and meekness.[104] Rogers did not want the matter intensified; he knew it could destroy the union. The same problem the Lexington churches experienced, the clerical privilege of administering the ordinances, occurred in other places. Questions about ordination of elders arose and a church in Washington County asked the advice of the editors of the *Messenger*. Did this privilege lay with the church or a presbytery and did those ordained by the church have the right to baptize? The editors replied, "We hope this subject, on which there has been much contention, may not be agitated among us. Let us bear with one another till we all come in the unity of the faith."[105]

Some of the dogmatism that arose detracted from the spirit of unity, especially in respect to baptism for the remission of sins. It overflowed into other areas and unless one could produce a "Thus saith the Lord" for his action, it was considered unpermissible. For example, one group would not dismiss with prayer after having the Lord's Supper since Jesus and the disciples left the room after singing a hymn. It was urged that this was the only proper way for dismissal.[106] Fortunately this spirit did not prevail among many of the churches.

The weekly observance of the Lord's Supper was slow in gaining recognition in some places. Campbell contended that no church was truly reformed until it observed the supper every first day of the week, but Stone was not prepared to go that far. He did believe the weekly observance proper, but maintained a similar position as on baptism for remission of sins; that it should not be the *sine qua non* of fellowship and that forbearance should be practiced. He wrote,

> I have no objection against breaking bread every Lord's day, where the church is unanimous; for as oft as you do it, do it in remembrance of Jesus; this neither forbids, nor positively enjoins weekly attention to it. Yet to make every first day's communion, a *sine quo non* of christian fellowship and union, is unauthorized by the scripture.[107]

Another problem that arose was the hymn book controversy. Campbell, Scott, Stone, and Johnson agreed to edit a hymn book together to consolidate the union, and planned to meet at a central location to select the hymns. While Johnson and Stone were waiting to hear from Campbell regarding the time and location, Scott went to Virginia and, with Campbell, made the selections and wrote the prefaces for the book. They entitled it "The Disciples Hymn Book," printed some proof sheets, and sent them to Stone and Johnson for corrections. When they saw the title "Disciples" instead of "Christian" and read the prefaces, they objected and determined to have nothing to do with it. They instructed Campbell to remove their names, but he replied that 6,000 sheets had already been printed and altering the hymn book would not be an easy task. Stone and Johnson then sent

Fleming to Campbell with instructions not to use their names unless he changed the title, removed the prefaces, and inserted some of the hymns from their former book. Campbell agreed to alter the title, but thought it would ruin the book to change the prefaces.[108]

The difficulty arose because Campbell had shipped some of the books to Scott in Cincinnati. Campbell altered the title on those still in his office, but Scott did not change the title on those he received. Scott sold these unaltered and they became issues of controversy.[109]

Those who have come to the verge of charging Campbell with malintentions designed to create problems for the union must take into account certain considerations. Barton Stone did not invest any money in this enterprise due to his financial condition. Campbell had one-third interest in it and it seems certain that Johnson and Scott each had one-third interest.[110] Therefore, two-thirds of the stock-holders liked the work as it stood, and changes would have to be financed from their pockets. The financial situation could very well be the reason why Scott did not change the title page on the copies he had received; the expense involved and the binding required may have prohibited Scott from doing this work in Cincinnati. Had Stone offered to pay for the changes, it may have been different.

The three men financing the book were former Reformers and it must be remembered that the name had been a bone of contention between Campbell and Stone. Had the book been issued by former Christians it almost passes without saying that it would have borne the title, "The Christian Hymn Book." The fact that Campbell was willing to change the title, and did so in copies issued from his office, shows that he had some concern for the Kentucky brethren. The blame for the unkept promise lies with Walter Scott.

This reduces the point of controversy to Scott and Campbell's action in making the choices without meeting with

Stone and Johnson as planned. A study into the activities of the men at this time, especially Campbell who was making plans for his tour to the east in 1835, may provide a justifiable answer. The convenience afforded Campbell of Scott's presence with the two of them putting up the majority of capital for the enterprise, might readily answer the question. West commented that "lesser men than Johnson and Stone would have ceased to cooperate with Walter Scott and Alexander Campbell for such high-handed conduct."[111] Some further study may indicate their conduct was not as "high-handed" as has been supposed.

True, Campbell did not always handle situations to the best interests of the union. His language about the union in his announcement of the brethren giving up their former speculations caused some ill feelings and one Kentuckian wrote him,

> This information, brother Campbell, was not exactly correct. I am happy to say that none were called upon to renounce their own speculations or to embrace those of others in order to the enjoyment of fellowship and union.[112]

He further admonished Campbell, "Let us all endeavor to be careful neither to say nor do anything to check the good work which is going on upon the principle for which we all contend.[113]

Campbell replied in his next issue that he had been misunderstood and explained himself more fully, adding that if his information was incorrect, he wished to be put in possession of the true facts.[114] He smoothed this over as easily as possible, commending Fleming for his virtues.

Neither would Campbell admit that the Christians were on a par with his movement, but continued to look upon them as breakers up of the soil for his reform to restore the "ancient order of things." As one historian has written, "When one studies this period he must feel that Mr. Stone surrendered much for the sake of union and that Mr. Campbell was not always as gracious as he should have been."[115]

One of the most ardent opposers was William Phillips, a Methodist clergyman near Lexington who published a poem entitled, "The Learned Camels; or Gospel in the Water." Rogers said that this poem misrepresented them and resolved "every thing into water." "It had its brief day, — & perished with the ephemerals of the time," said Rogers. The Methodists circulated the poem "by thousands, if not tens of thousands" and carried it from meeting to meeting for distribution.[116] Irregardless of the opposition and problems, the union brought many benefits which they could not have otherwise enjoyed.

Rogers, writing nearly thirty years after the union, said,

> We are, perhaps, too near the period of it, to see all its advantages. Without doubt it is a remarkable event, considering the circumstances of it. I hesitate not to say, it stands alone in the history of the Church.[117]

FRUITS OF THE UNION

Many advantages of the union could be cited by that time. It removed the jealousy between the two bodies and let them work together without ill feelings toward each other. This, in turn, brought numerous additions and proselytes into the churches; "thousands upon thousands." New churches sprang up and grew quickly due to their zeal. It was not uncommon to find members of both parties prevalent in many of the new churches that were established.[118] "This state of things," wrote Rogers, "has been brought about by union, and constant and untiring exertion."[119]

The greatest contribution the "Christians" gave the

Reformers was their evangelistic fervor. One writer has said,

> It is my own opinion that . . . had not the Christian Connection in-
> filtrated its fiery evangelism through the veins of Campbell's
> followers, his movement would not have succeeded as it did
> thereafter.[120]

The Reformers also made a contribution to the "Christians;"
an earnest study of the Bible and a plea for conformity to the
Word.[121] Thus each gave the other something it lacked.

Sending the two evangelists out showed them "the
wisdom of combined missionary effort to spread the
Gospel."[122] They met with such success that by 1835 more
evangelists were selected to go to the field. This practice of
cooperation was essential to union and the growth made during those first three eventful years. Without cooperation it
would have remained another local experiment.

In his latter years Rogers looked back with pride upon the
union and wrote,

> Where does history record the fact of two large bodies of religious
> people, who had been extremely hostile to each other — almost poles
> apart in their speculations — laying down all these, & in the true spirit
> of Christian faith & love, sacrificing them all upon the altar of truth &
> Union? O! it was a sublime spectacle! A glorious triumph of truth over
> error, of faith over opinion, of the spirit of the gospel over the spirit of
> party.
>
> Such was our Union. May it never be severed; but may its prin-
> ciples spread & triumph, until the Church shall be one, & the world
> shall be converted! Amen, & Amen.[123]

That is how it happened in Kentucky. But what of the
other states where groups of both bodies existed? Would
they unite also?

> We answer, if they are sincere in their profession, and destitute of a
> party spirit, they will undoubtedly unite. But, should all elsewhere act
> inconsistently with their profession, we determined to do what we
> are convinced is right in the sight of God.[124]

CHAPTER SUMMARY

Although Alexander Campbell did not personally participate in the union in Kentucky and many of the people thought the differences between the two bodies were too great, union in Kentucky succeeded. The work of Stone and Johnson in sharing the editorship of *The Christian Messenger* and the travels of the evangelists, Smith and Rogers, offered an example and a united front to the people. Some anxious moments occurred but the men dealt with these graciously and with a kind spirit and overcame many of the obstacles. While Campbell may not have been completely in favor of such a union at the time it happened he encouraged the men involved and bade the evangelists God speed. John Smith had to first convince his congregations that he had acted properly in uniting with the Christians before leading them into the union. Rogers, having moved in his thinking from the old Christian position regarding salvation to an acceptance of the Campbellian position, did not face such a difficulty with his own people and was able to get into the field ahead of Smith. Their work not only brought together many congregations but fostered a spirit of evangelism that produced a rapid growth in the churches during the three years they labored as evangelists. Only in Eastern Kentucky were there some Christian churches that remained out of the union.

---

1. John Augustus Williams, *Life of Elder John Smith* (Nashville: Gospel Advocate Company, 1956), p. 369.

2. *Ibid.*

3. Williams stated that Creath was present, but he denied it. He wrote, "I saw it stated in one of our periodicals, in either 1869 or 1870, that A. Campbell, Jacob Creath, sen., and Jacob Creath, jr., attended the meeting in Lexington, Kentucky, in January, 1832, at which the friends of B.W. Stone and A. Campbell were united. This is a mistake. I know certainly that neither of us attended the meeting, because at that time the feelings between the two parties were not cordial. I did not oppose the union of the two people, but then I was not cordial in it, neither were the other two men mentioned. I had other reasons for not attending it." From P. Donan, *Memoir of Jacob Creath, Jr.* (Cincinnati: R.W. Carroll and Company, 1872), p. 213.

4. Williams, p. 370.

5. *Ibid.*

6. *Ibid,* p. 371.

7. *Ibid,* pp. 372-373.

8. *Ibid,* p. 373.

9. *Ibid.*

10. *Ibid.*

11. Stone and Johnson, "Union of Christians," *The Christian Messenger,* Volume VI (January, 1832), p. 7.

12. Williams, p. 368.

13. Stone and Johnson, "Introduction," *The Christian Messenger,* Volume VI (January, 1832), p. 4.

14. *Ibid.*

15. *Ibid,* p. 6.

16. Quoted by Murch, *Christians Only,* p. 112.

17. Stone and Johnson, p. 7.

18. See footnote 3. Jacob Creath, Jr., stated in his *Memoirs* that Jacob Creath, Sr., did not attend the meeting, although Elley listed him as a participant. Elley was an eyewitness, from the construction of the letter, and reported the event immediately. Creath is writing much later in life, and while positive about himself, may have forgotten some of the facts of the case through the years. Possibly Creath, Sr., attended some, but not all, of the meetings.

19. Scott, "Extract of a Letter," *The Evangelist,* Volume I (February, 1832), pp. 30-31.

20. *Ibid.*

21. West, *Barton Warren Stone,* p. 150.

22. Richardson, p. 387.

23. A. Campbell, "The Christian Messenger," *The Millennial Harbinger,* Volume 1 (October, 1830), p. 474.

24. A. Campbell, "Religious News — Extracts from Letters," *The Millennial Harbinger,* Volume III (January, 1832), p. 29.

25. A. Campbell, "Campbellites Uniting with the Arians," *The Millennial Harbinger,* Volume III (January, 1832), p. 36.

26. *Ibid.*

27. *Ibid.*

28. *Ibid.*

29. *Ibid.*

30. A. Campbell, "The Christian Messenger," *The Millennial Harbinger,* Volume III (March, 1832), p. 138.

31. *Ibid,* p. 139. For evidence that Elley wrote similar letters to both editors, compare his letter in *The Evangelist,* Volume I, p. 166, with two letters referred to in *The Millennial Harbinger,* Volume III, pp. 411-412. Although the dates differed a few days, the content is quite similar. That Campbell had either heard from Elley or had the copy of *The Evangelist* in hand is apparent from not following the denomination of Reformer given in the *Messenger,* but the terminology used by Elley.

32. Scott, "Extract of a Letter," *The Evangelist,* Volume I (February, 1832), p. 30.

33. *Ibid,* p. 139.

34. *Ibid.*

35. *Ibid.*

36. "John Allen Gano's Biographical Notebook December, 1831-1861," p. 19.

37. A. Campbell, "Communicated for the Millennial Harbinger," *The Millennial Harbinger,* Volume III (April, 1832), p. 192. Letter from H.C.C. (Coon) from Lexington, Kentucky, dated February, 1832.

38. A. Campbell, "The Union," *The Millennial Harbinger,* Volume III (May, 1832), p. 195.

39. Williams, p. 378.

40. A. Campbell, "Progress of Reform," *The Millennial Harbinger,* Volume VI (November, 1835), p. 567.

41. Williams, p. 379.

42. *Ibid,* p. 380.

43. *Ibid.*

44. Rogers also preached to four congregations at this time. See the article by Campbell, "The Christian Messenger," p. 138.

45. John Rogers, *J.T. Johnson,* pp. 29-30.

46. *Ibid,* p. 30.

47. "Life and Times of John Rogers," p. 134. Also compare report from Rogers dated March 9, 1832, in *The Christian Messenger,* Volume VI, (March, 1832), pp. 91-92.

48. Report from Rogers dated March 9, 1832. *The Christian Messenger,* Volume VI (March, 1832), p. 104.

49. Stone and Johnson, "Good News Continued," *The Christian Messenger,* Volume VI, (April, 1832), p. 125.

50. "Life and Times of John Rogers," p. 134.

51. "Affairs at Georgetown," *The Millennial Harbinger,* Volume III (June, 1832), pp. 277-278.

52. Williams, pp. 389-392, and his report dated April 14, 1832, from Monticello, *The Christian Messenger,* Volume VI, (May, 1832), pp. 145-148, and a second report on page 158.

53. Letter from Rogers dated May 16, 1832, *The Christian Messenger,* Volume VI (July, 1832), pp. 218-219.

54. "Life and Times of John Rogers," p. 138.

55. John Rogers, *J.T. Johnson,* p. 57.

56. "Life and Times of John Rogers," pp. 137-138.

57. Letter from John Rogers dated May 28, 1832, *The Christian Messenger,* Volume VI (July, 1832), pp. 219-220.

58. Williams, pp. 398-399.

59. Letter from Thomas Smith dated June 7, 1832, *The Christian Messenger,* Volulme VI (July, 1832), p. 221.

60. "Correspondence," *The Evangelist,* Volume I (July, 1832), p. 166.

61. "Life and Times of John Rogers," p. 140, and Letter from T. Smith dated July 2, 1832, in *The Christian Messenger,* Volume VI (August, 1832), p. 247.

62. Letter from Rogers dated July 11, 1832, *The Christian Messenger,* Volume VI (August, 1832), pp. 247-248.

63. Williams, p. 401.

64. Report by Johnson, *The Christian Messenger,* Volume VI (September, 1832), pp. 284-285.

65. Letter from John Smith dated August 30, 1832, *The Christian Messenger,*

Volume VI (September, 1832), p. 268.

66. Report from Rogers dated October 23, 1832, *The Christian Messenger,* Volume VI (November, 1832), pp. 349-350.

67. "Life and Times of John Rogers," p. 128.

68. Williams, p. 381.

69. Stone and Johnson, "To the Editors," *The Christian Messenger,* Volume VI (March, 1832), p. 88.

70. *Ibid.*

71. Letter from John Rogers dated March 27, 1832, *The Christian Messenger,* Volume VI (April, 1832), p. 104.

72. Stone and Johnson, *The Christian Messenger,* Volume VI (September, 1832), p. 286. Also pp. 348-349.

73. John Rogers, *J.T. Johnson,* pp. 30-31.

74. "Life and Times of John Rogers," p. 96.

75. *Ibid,* p. 126.

76. *Ibid.*

77. Williams, p. 418.

78. Letter from J.W. Roberts dated June 25, 1832, *The Christian Messenger,* Volume VI (August, 1832), p. 248.

79. Rogers, *Autobiography of Stone,* p. 141.

80. Letter from J. McCarty dated July 7, 1832, *The Christian Messenger,* Volume VI (August, 1832), p. 248.

81. "Correspondence," *The Evangelist,* Volume I (September, 1832), p. 215.

82. Williams, p. 405.

83. Stone and Johnson, Report by Johnson. *The Christian Messenger,* Volume VI (October, 1832), p. 296.

84. "Christian Knowledge and Practice," *The Christian Messenger,* Volume VI (October, 1832), pp. 316-318.

85. "Progress of Reform," Letter from John McCall dated December 6, 1832, *The Millennial Harbinger,* Volume IV (February, 1833), p. 92.

86. Stone and Johnson, "Editors' Address," *The Christian Messenger,* Volume VII (January, 1833), p. 3.

87. Williams, p. 436.

88. *Ibid,* p. 374, and "Life and Times of John Rogers," p. 126.

89. "Life and Times of John Rogers," p. 174.

90. *Ibid.*

91. Rogers, *J.T. Johnson,* pp. 77-78.

92. "Progress of Reform," Letter from H.M. Bledsoe dated September 5, 1834, *The Millennial Harbinger,* Volume V (September, 1834), pp. 476-477.

93. *Ibid,* p. 477.

94. "John Allen Gano's Biographical Notebook," Typewritten copy in Lexington Theological Seminary library, Lexington, Kentucky, pp. 476-477.

95. N. Summerbell, *The Autobiography of Elder Matthew Gardner* (Dayton: Christian Publishing Association, 1875), p. 67.

96. *Ibid.*

97. Lamb, p. 107.

98. Williams, p. 381.

99. J.J. Summerbell, *Quadrennial Book of the American Christian Convention* (Dayton: Christian Publishing Association, 1886), pp. 86-89.

100. Letter from Matthew Gardner, *Christian Palladium,* Volume VI (May,

1837), p. 24.

101. Letter from A.M. Lansdown dated April 24, 1841, from Locust Creek, Kentucky, *Christian Palladium.* Volume X (June, 1841), p. 47.

102. Williams, p. 387.

103. Stone and Johnson, "Some Thoughs Addressed to the People, Called Christians in the West," *The Christian Messenger,* Volume VI, (April, 1832), p. 103.

104. John Rogers, "Some objections to the doctrine of Baptism for Remission of Sin, considered — in answer to a communication from Father Purviance," *The Christian Messenger,* Volume VII (March, 1833), pp. 76-77.

105. Letter from William Lambert dated January 4, 1834, from Washington County, Kentucky, *The Christian Messenger,* Volume VIII (January, 1834), pp. 29-30.

106. Williams, p. 422.

107. "The Conference in Terra Confusa," *The Christian Messenger,* Volume IX (July, 1835), p. 152.

108. B.W. Stone, "Answer to Bro. Thomas Carr's Letter," *The Christian Messenger,)* Volume IX (October, 1835), pp. 227-228.

109. *Ibid,* p. 226.

110. Since these were the only three men who had supplies of books for sale, it seems they were the financiers. "Psalms, Hymns, and Spiritual Songs," *The Millennial Harbinger,* Volume V (Mary, 1834), pp. 239-240.

111. West, p. 192.

112. "A Complaint," *The Millennial Harbinger,* Volume III (May, 1832), p. 238.

113. *Ibid.*

114. "Remarks on the Complaint," *The Millennial Harbinger,* Volume III (June, 1832), p. 279.

115. Fortune, p. 129.

116. "Life and Times of John Rogers," pp. 184-185.

117. *Ibid,* p. 127.

118. For example, in Russell County "nineteen Baptist brethren" united with the Christians in such a work. In Fleming County a new church began with individuals from each group as well as some Methodists and Tunkers. *The Millennial Harbinger,* Volume IV (March, 1833), pp. 140-141, and (October, 1833), p. 525.

119. Rogers, *J.T. Johnson,* p. 80.

120. Benjamin Lyon Smith, *Alexander Campbell,* (St. Louis: The Bethany Press, 1930), pp. 304-305.

121. Moore, p. 255.

122. Williams, p. 435.

123. "Life and Times of John Rogers," p. 127.

124. Williams, p. 375.

6

CONFLICT IN OHIO

INTRODUCTION

A different spirit prevailed in Ohio and the union efforts were not nearly as successful. Every conference of the Christian Church lost some churches to the unionists, but each one also emerged with some churches. The dialogue method followed in Kentucky turned to debate in Ohio. Bitter feelings toward each other were created that lasted for several years.

FANNING THE FLAMES OF ILL FEELINGS

"Sincere in profession" and "destitute of party spirit" were not descriptive adjectives for many in Ohio, where the greatest controversy, fueled by both sides, developed.[1] Some

Christians could not overcome various prejudices while many of the Reformers were extremists, creating an atmosphere of distrust and separatism.

Some charged Stone with forsaking the Christian Church and that *The Christian Messenger* was no longer "orthodox," leaving no alternative but to withdraw support. "It appears," wrote one correspondent from Ohio about the *Messenger,* "to favor the errors of the Reformers who are splitting and destroying our churches, and it has left us to contend alone."[2] Stone said he was occupying the same ground as always, except now he advocated some things more than in the past. The Reformers had some error, he admitted, but so did the Christians, and in uniting together as one body they had not agreed to receive each other's errors.[3]

Stone later expressed his feelings that much of the problem of effecting the union rested with the preachers.

> This union, I have no doubt, would have been as easily effected in other states as in Kentucky, had there not been a few ignorant, headstrong bigots on both sides, who were more influenced to retain and augment their party, than to save the world by uniting according to the prayer of Jesus.[4]

One of the Christian preachers who opposed the union, David Purviance, also put much of the blame on the preachers. Writing about Stone later in life he said,

> It is known that difficulties have existed, and some divisions have taken place in the church, in the latter part of his life; but I verily believe if all the preachers had been endued with as much of the wisdom that cometh from above as he possessed, a separation could not have been made.[5]

Abraham Snethen, the opposer of union along the Big Sandy in Kentucky, said as far as he was concerned, "there has never been a so-called union between the Disciples and the Christians except where the Christians adopt the

Disciples' peculiar doctrines and practices. . . ."[6] So some problems arose, obviously, over the system or method of union. The possibility of some deception existed since the editor of the *Presbyterian* gave an account, learned from a friend, of how the Reformers supposedly worked.

A shrewd follower of Campbell comes to a certain village where these errors are unknown. He at first calls himself a Baptist, and no one suspects the contrary. He professes great liberty of sentiment towards other denominations, preaches so as to please all, and appears full of zeal. After a little he announces that on such a day he will preach a sermon on Christian Union. At the appointed time he portrays in glaring colors the evils of sectarianism, and traces them all to creeds and confessions. He then proposes a plan in which all can unite, viz. — to lay aside all creeds and take the Scriptures as the only guide. The only question to be asked in order to church membership, is, "Do you believe that Jesus is the Christ; and are you willing to be governed by his law alone?" A simple affirmative is the only reply. At the close he commences in a whining tone to call on all who are willing to unite, to come forward. In the instance witnessed by our informant every Baptist who was present went forward. When this had taken place, the preacher began to declare what he called 'the ancient gospel' — simple belief that Jesus is the Christ — and then immersion for the remission of sins.[7]

Many opposers among the Christian preachers interpreted union as accepting Campbell's beliefs, which many were not prepared to do, citing their past "experiences" as different from what Campbell advocated.

Even in Kentucky many were fearful for the union at the end of the first year because of "the diversity of sentiment which still existed on the subject of baptism; . . ." and specifically, baptism for the remission of sins.[8] Rogers wrote on this vital subject in *The Christian Messenger,*

Some among us have embraced it cordially; others reject it. What then: Shall those who embrace it, condemn those who, tho' they believe in immersion, cannot go the whole length with us in this matter? God forbid. Or shall those who do not receive it, condemn those who do? I trust not. Charity forbids it. Our principles forbid it.[9]

In Ohio the subject developed into a full-scale war that lasted into the next decade.

The *Christian Palladium,* published in New York, became the journal for the disaffected Christian group. The editor, Joseph Badger, responding to an article advocating that only John was inspired to baptize, wrote, "Though we object to his Quaker sentiments on this point, we like them better than we do the opinions of Mr. Campbell, which makes baptism a door into the church. . . ."[10] B.H. Miles, a former preacher at Meigs County, Ohio, used the pages of the *Palladium* to speak out against baptism for remission of sins, calling it a "soul chilling doctrine."[11] Another Christian preacher, J.B. Hand, wrote to the *Palladium* in 1838,

> About five years ago, I was traveling the circuit of Clinton, Madison, Fayette and Pickaway counties, in this state, and the people who called themselves Disciples attended my meetings regularly, in many places, and pushed me into the water till I could find no bottom. I then got alarmed and began to look around, but could see no shore.[12]

Such journalism contributed nothing to the union. John Rogers, taking issue with Miles over his statements, requested the matter be discussed publicly through the pages of both *The Christian Messenger* and the *Palladium*. The editor of the *Palladium* refused.

So touchy became the issue that J.N. Perkins wrote from Williamsport, Ohio, saying that some of the Christian preachers "were afraid to name baptism lest they should be called Campbellites."[13]

While Campbell, Stone, and Johnson upheld the doctrine of baptism for the remission of sins in their periodicals, the pages of the *Palladium* were used against the doctrine. J. Marsh wrote a lengthy article listing six objections against the doctrine.

> 1st. *It makes the ways of God unequal.* For if there is *no other*

way in which *God* remits sin but in *baptism, He* has made it *possible* for some to be saved, while with others it is *literally impossible.* . . .

2d. *It stamps as spurious,* the many ten thousand experiences of all orders and no orders of christians . . . who *were not baptized for the remission of sins!!* . . . Hence the *holy* of all sects are *unchristianized* by this modern system of salvation!! But should it be said that the *experience* of the virtuous of all orders is *genuine,* this would at once *destroy* the idea that baptism is the only means for remission of sins. . . .

3d. *It makes baptism a door into the church* . . . Therefore . . . *a more holy,* and higher estimate is placed on the *character* of that person, who, but an *hour* or *two before* he was *baptized,* was one of the *vilest,* of the *vile,* than on the character of one who has *long* been strictly pious and fully devoted to the cause of his Redeemer, but was never *baptized.* . . .

4th. This doctrine represents *God, Christ,* and the *Holy Spirit,* as exercising no *power, influence,* or *agency* whatever in the salvation of the sinner, only what is produced by *the word.* . . .The sinner must *believe, reform,* and submit to *baptism,* and *all* can be performed within *five* minutes, and he comes out not only a good *disciple,* but fully qualified to administer all the ordinances of the house of God.

5th. The doctrine that baptism was instituted for the remission of sins, supercedes the neccessity of *prayer before* the forgiveness of sins. . . . Hence the numerous *precepts* and *examples* for the sinner to *pray before* his sins are remitted, are *all* set aside as useless. . . .

6th. This doctrine makes the confirming or *sealing evidence* of the remission of sins to consist in the *act* of the *creature,* not in the pardoning mercy of *Him* who alone can forgive sins.[14]

MATTHEW GARDNER AND
DAVID PURVIANCE OPPOSE UNION

Much of the rhetoric on the issue centered around Matthew Gardner in Southern Ohio. Problems surfaced in 1835 in Gardner's church at Georgetown over weekly observance of the Lord's Supper and electing bishops in the church; or, namely, "the restoration of the ancient order of things." James Clark wrote to John T. Johnson, now publishing the *Gospel Advocate,* stating that some had tried to get the church "into a primitive order," but Gardner, after two months recess, had a *"monthly meeting,* at which time he rallied the opposition and undertook to vote us down, to make the majority say we had no need of any other Elder than his *highness,* for he assumes to be HEAD of the church."[15] Johnson made some editorial comments, stating that Gardner was "capable of doing the cause of truth some little injury."

> He has already played off his *light* artillery upon us, at a *long shot,* away in the East. — He has been instrumental, as we are assured and believe, in alienating the affections of worthy and amiable brethren from each other; and has excited a spirit of faction in the congregation alluded to.[16]

Gardner responded to the letter and the editorial comments, claiming Clark's party set up weekly communion nearly two years before without consulting the church, yet no one objected if they did not infringe on the privileges of those who saw no need for it. He said the real problem centered in selection of bishops without giving notice to the other members of the church not of Clark's party, and Clark was one chosen to become a bishop. At the regular meeting of the church the question was placed before them "whether the church wished those brethren who had been chosen by a part of the church to serve them as Bishops,"[17] and it was voted down. The controversy led to a separation in the church at Georgetown.

Gardner challenged Johnson or any other respectable teacher of the reformation to a debate, agreeing to accept the negative of the proposition "that God has instituted immersion, to be joined with faith and repentance, in order to, or by, or through, which mankind are to obtain remission of sins, and the Holy Spirit."[18]

The controversial Gardner continued writing against what he termed "Campbellism." He published a twenty-four page pamphlet, in 1835 entitled, "Twelve Years Observation and

Examination of Mr. Alexander Campbell's Theory and Practice of Reformation.''[19] When a copy of this came to Campbell, he acknowledged it, but refused to address any of the issues, saying that Gardner's character had been questioned and he would not answer such a man. Gardner thought the charges against his character were unfairly treated by the Reformers and wrote later in life that ''all the abuse heaped upon me by the Campbellites did not diminish my congregations.''[20] On one occasion a Reformer deacon attended Gardner's church and confronted him after the services. As the preacher attempted to walk around him to leave, the deacon struck Gardner, then clenched his hand into his ''collar'' and refused to let go, even at the request of friends. It ended with the local law imposing a fine upon the deacon.[21]

Gardner said the union consisted of the Christians ''. . . receiving the system of doctrine, and adopting the new practice, modes, and forms of the disciples.''[22] He regretted his separation from former friends and expressing these feelings he wrote,

> When Elder B.W. Stone and other dear brethren went over to Mr. C's views, I tried to reconcile the Scriptures to this system, for it was afflicting to me to think of being separated from those who I had been with so long. But I found if I received Mr. C's theory I must deny my experience, the evangelical power of religion and the plain word of the Lord. When the subject was thus presented to my mind, it did not take me long to decide.[23]

He remained an opponent of the union to the end of his life.

David Purviance, one of the signers of *The Last Will and Testament of the Springfield Presbytery* with Stone, but now living in Ohio, also refused to enter into union. He maintained the ground of the old Christians; that Christian character should be the sole test of Christian fellowship. He believed that immersion was proper, but would not reject from fellowship those who were not immersed. He never accepted the doctrine of baptism for the remission of sins, but had confidence in the honesty and piety of many who did.[24]

DEBATES IN OHIO

A number of debates took place between the Reformers and the Christians. Matthias Winans and Nathan Mitchell of the Reformers and Enoch Harvey and Alexander McClain of the Christians debated at Jamestown in 1836. The Christians had used the building of the Reformers in Jamestown for a revival, with the stipulation that at the end any differences would be discussed. When asked if anything occurred unscriptural, Winans brought up the issue of the mourners' bench. Harvey asked if he wanted to debate it and Winans answered affirmatively. The proposition was "Faith, repentance and baptism precede the remission of sins under the gospel dispensation."[25] It appears from the scanty records that Mitchell and McClain were the speakers.

The proposition that Gardner offered to John T. Johnson in 1835 became the focal point of a debate in Jamestown, Ohio, between Gardner and J.B. Lucas of the Reformers on June 9 and 10, 1839. Lucas took the affirmative and Gardner the negative.[25] The same men debated again in October, 1840, at Lebanon.

Another debate on principally the same proposition was conducted between Dr. W. Belding and Lucy of the Disciples and James Hayes of the Christians in 1841 at Guilford and Hanover, Ohio.[26]

Other debates hindered union in Ohio. Elisha Ashley, a Christian preacher ordained in 1823, said, "The first thing I came in contact with was Campbellism, and I had several debates on that subject."[27]

WRONG ATTITUDES

Another major cause for failure in Ohio was the attitudes of many of the Reformers. Some publicly and very zealously contended that non-Christians should not pray nor should Christians pray for them. Some preachers would not even pray for guidance to invoke the Spirit's direction when preaching the Word. Such overreaction to the mourners' benches of the Christians damaged the cordial feelings of many.[28] This spirit produced a stiffness that left some of the former Christians feeling cold. Samuel Rogers was quoted as saying,

> We Newlights were so anxious to have all Christians united that when we saw the Baptists making a move for union, we, in our haste to meet them, ran clear through the temperate zone and joined them in the frigid zone; but we hoped we would get back to the true gospel zone after awhile.[29]

Rogers also said he feared that in casting out the mourners' bench they had also cast out the mourners.

A correspondent to Campbell complained of some "faults" deterring the growth of the church,

> . . . such as bad preaching, such as abusing the sects, and unsound doctrine in respect to the Spirit — such as contending that there was no other Spirit than the Word. This we did not believe. On some occasions our hearts have almost ceased to palpitate. We grew cold and lifeless; but thank our heavenly Father, we have recovered from the shock, and are now quite healthy.[30]

Stone noted this attitude also in Ohio.

> Faith without works is dead; faith in the scriptures without the Spirit of that book in the heart, and manifest in holiness of life, is not that faith which unites according to the prayer of Jesus. This we see exemplified in some of the Ohio churches. They all profess to take the word of God for the alone foundation of their faith and practice; but now are divided, and the tocsin of a new religious war is heard afar. It

151

is a pity that the bruit(sic) of such a war had not been confined to that state and not sent abroad in pamphlets to the shame of christians, and the laugh of infidels. The provoking language of bullies is used in those writings instead of that of conciliation. What better evidence do we need that such have not the spirit of the Bible?[31]

OHIO SOUTHERN CONFERENCE

One historian stated that the union in Kentucky "had but little if any effect in Ohio."[32] That statement needs greater clarification for hardly a single Christian conference in Ohio was left unscathed by the efforts of union. The Ohio Southern Conference (Matthew Gardner's conference), encompassing Clermont, Adams, Brown, Hamilton, and Highland Counties had serious problems. Georgetown and Bethel both split. Liberty (Brown County) and Lawshe, as well as others, came under the influence of the union group.[33] The conference meetings in 1836 found only Matthew Gardner and Alexander McClain as preachers in good standing. Three others, John Powell, Alonzo Knowles, and Otho Perre withdrew under censure and refused to answer charges against them and "all privileges, rights, and advantages, whether religious or by law, granted to them by the c. church, are hereby declared null and void."[34] The principal issue appears to be that these men had accepted Reformer views. Gardner later wrote, "When I heard the cry for union coming from these men, I knew the design was to break up the churches, or to carry them over to Discipleism."[35] When the conference met in 1837 only Gardner and McClain were listed as preachers among nine churches who reported a total membership of 866. The correspondent, Mark Briney from the Miami Conference who served as clerk, appended this note to his report to the *Palladium*.

It is well known to you that a majority of the preachers in this conference have gone over into Mr. Campbell's reform; yet Elders Gardner and McClain have so successfully combatted the power of darkness, that about ONE THOUSAND members are well satisfied to marshall under the banner of Christian liberty; . . .[36]

Gardner was responsible, in 1863, for keeping the two bodies from uniting in Ripley. A Disciples preacher, after preaching for a week, set an appointment for uniting the two groups. Gardner went to the meeting and pointed out the differences; namely (1) women were not permitted equal privileges in Disciples' churches, (2) only the immersed were accepted in full fellowship by the disciples, and (3) weekly communion. He advised consideration before entering it and the union attempt failed.[37]

MIAMI CONFERENCE AND SURROUNDING AREA

The Miami Conference, encompassing at least Shelby, Miami, Darke, Clarke, Green and Preble Counties, also experienced severe problems. The conference passed a resolution in 1838 against Reformer doctrine being preached in their churches.[38] The church at Troy divided because of the Reformer doctrines,[39] while others lost members in 1834,[40] but a few years later it was reported that in this area "Several preachers of the Christian Church have united with the Reformers and are doing all they can to oppose the practices of our society," among whom was Henry Monfort of Eaton.[41] The church in New Paris (Preble County) had lost a large number of members to the Reformers.[42] Benjamin Alton, another preacher working in the boundaries of this conference, "went over to Mr. Campbell, and took the little few with him. . . ."[43]

Further erosion of the Christian Church in this area is stated in a letter from Lebanon, Ohio, in 1838, to the *Palladium.*

. . . we think if the churches had taken a decided stand in the outset, with a fixed and determined resolution to mark all who would cause divisions or offences, hundreds, yes hundreds could have been prevented from being swallowed up by that cold, dead, lifeless system called reform; and we think there could be something done in this way yet. But no, says the minister to his congregation, there is but a shade of difference between us and them; we will form a union. Well, this was done in different places: we forbear mentioning names; . . .[44]

OHIO CENTRAL CONFERENCE

The Ohio Central Conference, which probably included Clinton, Madison, Champaign, Logan, Union, Delaware, Licking, Franklin, Pickaway, Knox and Fayette Counties, remained relatively free of any problems except on their fringes.[45] The conference reported forty-two churches ranging in membership from eight to seventy-eight at their meeting in Knox County on August 20, 1834.[46] Their camp meeting in Licking County started on Sunday, August 22, with an estimated attendance of 7,000 people.[47] In 1837, Isaac Walters reported that the conference had twenty-two elders and nine secretaries "and none of them tinctured with, or at all favorable to Campbellism."[48] The problems in this conference were in Clinton County to the southwestern edge and in Licking County to the east. John Hamrick reported that in Clinton County he had to stand almost alone "against the current of water salvation."[49] Samuel Rogers had started Christian churches in this area, but went the route of the Reformers after hearing Campbell speak. According to Rogers there were "two or three old brethren that had stood out against the Reformation" in this area. He thought they would have yielded had it not been for "a few mischief-making spirits, who made periodical visits to the neighborhood for the purpose of stirring up strife, and reviving the prejudices of the few remaining disaffected ones."[50] He returned to the area in

1839, having left there in 1833, and held a two weeks protracted meeting. During the meeting the three men came forward and "confessing their errors, asked to be admitted to the fellowship of the church."[51] So very little ground was left for the old Christians in Clinton County.

Licking County Christian churches were in a state of growth until "the soul chilling doctrines of discipleism . . . spread its baneful influence among us,"[52] according to a correspondent from Granville, Ohio, brought in by men who held standing in the Christian Church. Some obviously entered the union from the statement, "But I feel thankful to say that a few churches and brethren have weathered the storm. . . ."[53]

Garrison states that the Bethany Reformers had not yet reached this region of central Ohio and as a result, the "Bible Christians" maintained their original distinct identity in that area.[54] With the exception of the two fringe areas where the Reformers had some effective works, his statement is true. The Central Ohio Conference did remain the strongest and least affected.

OHIO EASTERN CONFERENCE

To the southeast was the Ohio Eastern Conference which emerged with several "Bible Christian" churches intact. While some of the counties in the area were not aligned with this conference they apparently had no conference affiliation and later were added. This included the counties of Gallia, Meigs, Washington, Monroe, Noble, Morgan, Athens, Hocking and Perry. William McCaslin did much to keep the conference together, along with Elder McDonald, when many were leaving and joining the Disciples.[55] McCaslin, McDonald, and E. Shaw wrote to the editor of the *Palladium* in 1839 deploring the conditions of the churches as a result of Reformer influence.

> We are situated in the counties of Perry, Morgan, and Athens, Ohio; and were once united in a harmonious and prosperous conference, but the disorganizing influence of Mr Campbell's theory, has thrown confusion and moral death into our once peaceful ranks, which has nearly proved our destruction, as a people; and we expect we are now little known in the Christian connexion. Yet there are many who have not fallen prey to the delusions of the time. — We have six small churches, which would probably number about two hundred members. . . .[56]

Meigs and Gallia Counties came through the turmoil with several Christian churches, although one correspondent wrote that "Campbellism has prevailed here,"[57] indicating it did have its day. Several Bible Christian congregations still exist in these counties although one of these congregations, Columbia Chapel Christian Church in Meigs County, left the conference in 1961 to become a part of the group that formed the union.

OTHER CONFERENCES

Two other conferences, Scioto in the south central and Ohio Union in the northwestern sector of the state, seemed to have fewer problems. Elder Joseph Baker wrote in 1838 that among all the ministers and churches in the Scioto conference "there is not the smallest jar of division."[58]

One of the most interesting conferences was Salt Creek which, in 1835, reported ten preachers, twenty-five churches, and 925 members. The report stated, "Elder Baker is striving hard to end the division between the followers of Jesus Christ and the adherents of Mr. Campbell's doctrine."[59] Baker leaned toward the sentiments of Campbell and had a lasting effect on this conference which united with the Disciples in 1933, a century after the Kentucky union.

Stone surely identified Ohio when he said that there were headstrong bigots on both sides.

CHAPTER SUMMARY

The union in Ohio faced many obstacles that prohibited it from being as successful as in Kentucky. The spirit and attitude of some preachers on both sides contributed to the failure. Some thought that Stone had forsaken them and *The Christian Messenger* had become an organ for Campbellism. They turned to the eastern Christians for support and subscribed to their journal, the *Christian Palladium,* which championed the cause of the disaffected Christians in the west. The doctrine of immersion for remission of sins was the focal point for much of the controversy. It was discussed publicly and privately in their journals and debated heavily, with Matthew Gardner offering the most opposition. Not a single conference of the Christian Church in Ohio went unscathed as each lost churches to the union. Only the Ohio Central Conference remained relatively intact.

---

1. Williams, *Life of Elder John Smith,* p. 376.

2. Letter from J.M. of Hamilton County, Ohio. *The Christian Messenger,* Volume VII (January, 1833), p. 3.

3. Stone, "Reply," *Ibid,* p. 4-6.

4. Ware, *B.W. Stone,* p. 272.

5. Rogers, *Biography of B.W. Stone,* p. 129.

6. Lamb, p. 191.

7. "From the 'Presbyterian,' " *The Millennial Harbinger,* Volume IV (May, 1833), p. 227.

8. Williams, p. 414-415.

9. John Rogers, "Some thoughts addressed to the people, called christians in the West," *The Christian Messenger,* Volume VI (April, 1832), p. 103.

10. Joseph Badger, *The Christian Palladium,* Volume V (April, 1837), p. 377.

11. Rogers, "Life and Times of John Rogers," p. 149.

12. Humphreys, *Deceased Ministers* p. 155.

13. Letter from J.N. Perkins, *Christian Palladium,* Volume X (June, 1841), p. 63.

14. J. Marsh, "Facts are Stubborn Things," *Christian Palladium,* Volume III (March, 1835), pp. 330-331 and (April, 1835), pp. 348-349.

15. Letter from James Clark, *Gospel Advocate,* Volume I, p. 77.

16. J.T. Johnson, "Anti-Sectarian-Sectarianism," *Ibid,* p. 76. The comments had reference to Gardner's remarks in the *Christian Palladium.*

17. Letter from Matthew Gardner dated June 6, 1835, *Gospel Advocate,* Volume I, p. 126.

18. *Ibid,* p. 127.

19. "Elder Gardner's Conclusions," *Christian Palladium,* Volume IV (November 1, 1835), p. 203.

20. N. Summerbell, editor, *The Autobiography of Matthew Gardner* (Dayton: Christian Publishing Association, 1874), p. 77.

21. Letter from Gardner dated July 28, 1836, *Christian Palladium,* Volume V (September 1, 1836), p. 138. Compare also N. Summerbell, p. 77.

22. Summerbell, p. 74.

23. Letter from Gardner dated March 1, 1836, *Christian Palladium,* Volume IV, (April 20, 1836), p. 371.

24. Levi Purviance, *The Biography of Elder David Purviance,* (Dayton: B.F. & G. Wells, 1848), pp. 80-81.

25. Letter from J.O. Harris dated June 24, 1839, *Christian Palladium,* Volume VIII (August 15, 1839), p. 126. See also Summerbell, p. 80 for Lebanon debates.

26. *Christian Palladium,* Volume X (November, 1841), p. 222.

27. Humphreys, p. 27-28.

28. Williams, p. 376.

29. Belle Stanford, *Autobiography and Sermons of Elder Elijah Martindale* (Indianapolis: Carlon and Hollenbeck, Printers, 1892), p. 28.

30. Letter from Leroy Lemert dated December 7, 1835, *Millennial Harbinger,* Volume VII (January, 1836), p. 35.

31. B.W. Stone, "Reformation," *The Christian Messenger,* Volume IX (December, 1835), p. 267.

32. Henry K. Shaw, *Buckeye Disciples: A History of the Disciples of Christ in Ohio* (St. Louis: Christian Board of Publication, 1952), p. 19.

33. Lamb, p. 12.

34. "Minutes of Ohio Southern Christian Conference," *Christian Palladium,* Volume V (October, 1836), p. 198.

35. Summerbell, pp. 74-75.

36. "Ohio Southern Conference," *Christian Palladium,* Volume VI (November, 1837), p. 203.

37. Summerbell, pp. 74-75.

38. "Minutes of the Ohio Miami Conference," *Christian Palladium,* Volume VI (November, 1838), p. 223.

39. Letter from Alexander McCullough dated September 29, 1840, *The Christian Messenger,* Volume XI (December, 1840), p. 126.

40. Letter from D. Millard dated February 3, 1834, *Christian Palladium,* Volume II (March, 1834), pp. 351-352.

41. "Extract from the Recent Journal of Elder Isaac N. Walters in Ohio," *The Christian Messenger,* Volume XII (March, 1842), p. 157.

42. *Ibid.*

43. Letter from Thomas Mumford dated July 15, 1837, *Christian Palladium,* Volume VI (August, 1837), p. 124.

44. J.T. Nixon, "Western Reform," *Christian Palladium,* Volume VII (August, 1838), p. 100.

45. It is difficult to identify exact boundaries of the Ohio conferences. I have listed counties that were in the boundaries of the conferences at a later date to help the reader get a grasp on the possible areas.

46. "The Ohio Central Conference," *Christian Palladium,* Volume III (December, 1834), p. 239.

47. A.L. McKinney, *Memoir of Isaac N. Walter,* (Cincinnati: Rickey, Mallory & Webb, 1857), p. 118.

48. "Elder I.N. Walter's Journal," *Christian Palladium,* Volume VI (November, 1837), p. 199.

49. Letter from John Hamrick dated April 2, 1838, *Christian Palladium,* Volume VII (May, 1838), p. 27.

50. J.I. Rogers, p. 153.

51. *Ibid,* p. 154.

52. Letter from E. Williamson dated May 9, 1839, *Christian Palladium,* Volume VIII (June, 1839), p. 44.

53. *Ibid.*

54. Garrison, *The Reformation of the Nineteenth Century,* p. 91.

55. Humphreys, p. 22.

56. Letter from Elders J. McDonald, E. Shaw, and W. McCaslin dated January 11, 1839, *Christian Palladium,* Volume VII (April, 1839), p. 379-380.

57. Letter dated April 20, 1827, *Christian Palladium,* Volume VI (June, 1837), p. 41.

58. Letter from Elder Joseph Baker dated November 28, 1838, *Christian Palladium,* Volume VII (January, 1839), p. 271.

59. "Summary," *Christian Palladium,* Volume III (April, 1835), p. 372.

7

THE NEIGHBOR STATES TO KENTUCKY

INTRODUCTION

Fortunately the union went smoother in most other border states than in Ohio. Indiana experienced similar difficulties but only minor problems prevailed elsewhere. Virginia had several Christian Churches who aligned themselves with the eastern Christians who did not enter the union, but Tennessee, Illinois, and Missouri had good success.

TENNESSEE

"In Tennessee, the union of the two groups went smoothly. It should not have been otherwise, there were few congregations to merge."[1] The Christians numbered approximately 4,000 members in 60 churches with 32 preachers.[2] The Reformers had perhaps 10 congregations.[3]

Union began in Tennessee almost immediately after the first union meetings in Kentucky. In Griffith County, on January 4, 1832, the

> . . . members of the Church of Christ, and . . . the Reformed Baptists regardless of all charges about Trinitarianism, Arianism, and Socinianism, and of questions whether it is possible for any person to get to heaven without immersion, or whether immersion is for the remission of sins, have come forward, given the right hand of fellowship, and united upon the plain and simple Gospel.[4]

Reports of union in other counties came to the editors of *The Christian Messenger*. A correspondent from McNairy County gave a very descriptive account of events there.

> Those who are called . . . Campbellites and the christians, are friendly. We are united in spirit, and generally in form. We preach, pray, sing, and commune together. We join in all social acts of worship together — unitedly labor to reform the world. Opinions are mutually held as private property.[5]

Union in Rutherford County came at a camp meeting on the last Lord's day in July, 1832, where the two groups formally united. A rather large group attended since it was reported during the meeting that the fruits of the union were 82 immersed.[6] Letters from Maury County and Williamsport stated that the groups were uniting in those communities.[7] By early 1833 the merger was nearly completed.

Two minor problems surrounded the union which apparently had little effect on success; the selection of a name and some of the customs of the Christians that tended to linger. When it came to selecting a name, spokesmen were there for "Disciples of Christ," "Reformers," "Church of Christ," and "Christian Church," with the latter prevailing.[8] William Willeford wrote from Wilson County to Campbell in

1836 reproving the Christians for some of their former ways that some were still practicing.

> I have nearly lost all hope of the cause of reform that you and other brethren plead for, ever advancing much amongst that body of people who call themselves christians in this section, and who belong to the same people that united with our brethren in Kentucky and elsewhere some since that time.[9]

He accused the Christians of admitting "moral men" into their fellowship, apparently an allusion to accepting people without immersion, only meeting once a month for worship, and taking the Lord's supper only once a year.

> Brother Campbell, these same people talk much about union. They seem to forget that a strict compliance with all the commandments of the Lord Jesus Christ, as written in the New Testament, is the only foundation for his followers to unite upon. . . . So, my brother, I want nothing to do with any union but such a one as will be formed by uniting upon the New Testament and heartily doing whatever is commanded therein.[10]

These problems did not halt union in Tennessee.

INDIANA

Shaw summarizes the successful union work in Indiana by identifying the Christian preachers who worked for union. He wrote,

> Beginning about 1830 and continuing for about eight years, local New Light churches under the influence of such preachers as J.M. Mathes, Michael and Job Combs, Elijah Martindale, James Hughes of Kentucky, John Secrest of Ohio, Elijah Goodwin, Beverly Vawter, Love H. Jamieson and John O'Kane went completely into the Disciples movement.[11]

Some of these men worked successfully for union in some of

the churches prior to 1832. John O'Kane served during 1832 as evangelist in Rush, Fayette, and Decatur Counties where he was influential. Martindale traveled in Henry, Wayne, Fayette, Rush, Delaware, Madison, and Hancock Counties where he helped build up many of the Christian churches and succeeded in bringing most of them into union.[12] Elijah Goodwin did not accept Reformer doctrine until 1837 when he read *The Millennial Harbinger* while running a store. He continued reading in 1838 and became convinced that "our whole converting machinery was wrong."[13] He then took several of the churches into "Gospel order," including Union, Yankee Settlement near Mount Vernon, and later, Coffee Creek. Until 1840, according to Goodwin, none of the Reformer preachers had entered that section of the state.[14]

The largest union in Indiana occurred in Morgan County in 1833. Michael Combs went into Bartholomew County on business and learned about Jo. Fassett, a New Light preacher at New Hope church. He attended services at New Hope and found Elder Fassett an earnest advocate of union. They immediately began planning to unite the Reformers and the New Lights of Bartholomew and surrounding counties, organizing a meeting in August, 1833, at the bluffs of White River in Morgan County.[15]

Hundreds attended the meeting, including about ten preachers from each party. They agreed that the preachers of each group should speak "a few times alternately in order that the differences between the parties might be made manifest."[16] Elder Fasset spoke first on Friday morning and the meeting continued with alternating speakers until Monday evening.

> Both parties having renounced all human creeds, and both preaching for doctrine the Scripture given by inspiration of God, there appeared no material difference between them. All the speakers seemed to be of the same judgement, and to all speak the same thing. As early as Lord's day, it was evident that there were to be no more divisions be-

tween those two bodies of Christians. Hundreds sat down together that day at the table of their common Lord. . . . [17]

They set three cooperative meetings to follow; one in February at Greensburg, another near Crawfordsville in March and a final one in April at Indianapolis.[18]

The New Lights in the Bloomington area had a camp meeting scheduled in 1833 in Monroe County and invited Michael Combs to attend. Some Kentucky preachers, including John Smith, were supposed to be present but were unable to attend. Combs was asked to preach and that marked the beginning of the work for union in that county. Evans wrote (1862), "So well has the work commenced, and so successfully has it been prosecuted, that now there is not a single congregation — perhaps not a single member — of the Old Christian body in Monroe County."[19]

Still not all was well in Indiana; war existed there as in Ohio, although not as severe. Martindale, reviewing this period of time later in life, placed much of the blame on the preachers.

> They failed to exhibit the meekness and gentleness, the long forbearance that we should feel toward the erring. They cut off the ears of their hearers before the truth could reach their hearts. When the wall of prejudice has become so great it can only be removed by love. The war would never have been waged so intensely if our people had dwelt less on first principles and more on vital godliness and the indwelling of the Holy Spirit. Then it seems to me we could have helped them to get out of their ignorance and blindness.[20]

Some of the Christian preachers in Indiana who did not unite were George Alkire, Thomas Carr, Joseph Wasson, James Stackhouse, Joshua Selby, Silas Parks, John Plummer, John McCreary, William Lowe, Jess Hughs, Isaac Jessup, David Douglas, Isam Adkinson, and David McGahey.

McGahey published a pamphlet warning against Campbellism, advocating that a plan should be designed to detect heresies and keep them out of the church. The pamphlets were widely distributed throughout Indiana, creating a great amount of discussion and agitation. Elijah Goodwin wrote a review of it, but some opposed publishing it, fearful it would not help the situation.[21]

Because of the turmoil in their churches the Indiana Conference appointed two extra sessions in 1838 for the purpose of selecting and appointing two men to travel through the state to "set things in order where the disorganizing spirit has been."[22]

In Indiana, as in Ohio, several Christians stayed outside the merger. Later records list nine conferences of the Christian Church in that state.

ILLINOIS

Barton W. Stone made a tour into Illinois in 1832 and successfully brought together the Christians and Reformers in Jacksonville. Two other nearby towns, Carrolton and Jersey Prairie, were to follow with the same action the following Sunday. Stone moved to Jacksonville in 1834 and found the Christians and Reformers divided. He refused to unite with either group until they united, and his influence brought them together.[23]

One historian stated that after Stone moved to Illinois, a wave of Campbellism followed that "swept the Christians off their feet, and aggregated about eight thousand accessions to the Disciples."[24] Haynes supports this, stating that the Disciples absorbed the larger part of the "Christian Denomination" in Illinois.[25]

MISSOURI

Numerous reports were sent to both *The Christian Mes-*

senger and *The Millennial Harbinger* from Missouri telling of union and harmony between the two groups. From all indications the preachers were responsible for the harmony, many of them moving to Missouri from Kentucky having roots in the Stone movement there. The Rogers brothers had made an early tour into Missouri in the 1820's establishing contact between the Kentucky Christians and Missouri. When Samuel Rogers made this third tour to Missouri he found that all the congregations he encountered had come "fully into the light of Apostolic Christianity, though in and around Franklin they were much discouraged, having but one preacher in the entire district. . . ."[26]

The success of the union can be judged from later records of the Christian conferences in Missouri. In 1886 only three conferences were listed with only two making reports, listing a total of eight churches and 155 members.[27]

VIRGINIA

While many of the Christians in Virginia aligned themselves with the eastern Christians in New York, others were influenced by Stone's writings and visits from western Christian preachers. In Shenandoah and Hampshire Counties a merger was effected between many of the Christians and the Reformers in Eastern Virginia. James Ferguson and Christy Sine were the leading influences in this merger, resulting in a significant portion of the Christians uniting with the Reformers.[28]

Chester Bullard, a somewhat controversial preacher in Giles, Monroe, Montgomery, and Roanoke Counties, was the leading influence for union in that area of Virginia. Although he was baptized by Landon Duncan, a Christian preacher, he never totally subscribed to the doctrine of the Christians. This led to a conflict and a short separation from Duncan and

Parker Lucas in 1836. Bullard learned of the proximity of his views to Campbell and began correspondence with the Reformers of Eastern Virginia. Duncan and Lucas were cooperating with the Reformers by this time, leading to a reconciliation as union came. The result was that "virtually all the Christians in Monroe, Giles, Montgomery, Pulaski, Roanoke, and what was to become Craig Counties had become a part of the Virginia Brotherhood of Disciples."[29]

In Holston and Watauga Valleys union was effected by 1833 with nearly all the Christians of the conference in this area fusing with the Reformers.[30]

OTHER STATES

Except for the eastern states where the Eastern Christians were influential, the other states, particularly the south, had small groups of Christians and Reformers, yet union generally prevailed. Union with the Christians in the east never materialized, although Stone had hoped it would. New York, with several strong preachers and the *Christian Palladium* headquartered there, provided a solid base for them. They had members throughout the east and the disaffected in Ohio, Indiana, Illinois, and elsewhere aligned with them.

---

1. Herman A. Norton, *Tennessee Chrisians* (Nashville: Reed and Company, 1971), p. 28.

2. Letter from James E. Matthews dated September 10, 1831, *The Christian Messenger,* Volume V (December, 1831), pp. 280-281.

3. Norton, p. 28.

4. Williams, pp. 375-376.

5. Letter from M.N. Matthews dated April 11, 1832, *The Christian Messenger,* Volume VI (May, 1832), pp. 157-158.

6. Letter from E. Sweat, *Ibid,* (November, 1832), p. 345.

7. Letter from Barry Moore, *The Christian Messenger,* Volume VI (December, 1832), p. 378 and letter from William Cowden, *Ibid,* Volume VII (May, 1833), p. 156.

8. Norton, p. 29

9. Letter from William E. Willeford dated April 9, 1836, *The Millennial Harbinger,* Volume VII (May, 1836), p. 238.
10. *Ibid.*
11. Henry K. Shaw, *Hoosier Disciples* (St. Louis: The Bethany Press, 1966), p. 69.
12. Belle Stanford, pp. 32-33.
13. James Mathes, *Life of Elijah Goodwin, the Pioneer Preacher* (St. Louis: John Burns, Publisher, 1880), p. 134.
14. *Ibid,* pp. 137, 139-140, 189.
15. Madison Evans, *Biographical Sketches of the Pioneer Preachers of Indiana* (Philadelphia: J. Challen and Sons, 1862), pp. 150-151.
16. *Ibid,* p. 151.
17. *Ibid.*
18. Letter from Michael Combs dated January 15, 1834, *The Christian Messenger,* Volume VIII (February, 1834), p. 63.
19. Evans, p. 152.
20. Stanford, pp. 32-34.
21. Mathes, pp. 100-101.
22. "Indiana Conference Resolves Against Reform," *Christian Palladium,* Volume VII (October, 1838), p. 173.
23. B.W. Stone, *The Christian Messenger,* Volume VI (November, 1832), p. 347.
24. Milo True Morrill, *A History of the Christian Denomination in America, 1794-1911 A.D.* (Dayton: The Christian Publishing Association, 1912), p. 304.
25. Nathaniel Haynes, *History of the Disciples of Christ in Illinois, 1819-1914* (Cincinnati: Standard Publishing Company, 1915), p. 30.
26. John I. Rogers, p. 161.
27. J.J. Summerbell, *Quadrennial Book of the American Christian Conference* (Dayton: Christian Publishing Association, 1886), p. 86.
28. H. Jackson Darst, *Ante-Bellum Virginia Disciples* (Richmond: Virginia Christian Missionary Society, 1959), p. 22.
29. *Ibid,* pp. 28-30.
30. *Ibid,* p. 32.

CONCLUSION

HOW SOME HISTORIANS HAVE EVALUATED THE UNION

Historians among the Disciples have evaluated the union differently. W.T. Moore thought that from the Campbellian position the union had drawbacks, coming at a time when the Reformers were sweeping everything in front of them in the Baptist Churches in Kentucky and making inroads in other places. The union caused the Baptists, who considered the movement a reformation of the wrongs in their churches, to change that view, especially since some of the Christians were Paido-baptist in thinking.[1] The Baptists declared that the "*Campbellites* have made the gulf between us impassable by throwing themselves into the arms of the Arians."[2] Campbell also regretted splitting with the Baptists. He said,

I have always regretted that we and the Baptists had to part. It ought never to have been. I hoped that we and that great people could have stood together for the advocacy of apostolic Christianity. They are a great people, and worthy of such a mission.[3]

The question arises regarding the degree of success Campbell could have continued to have among the Baptists. By this time some strong leaders among them were beginning to take issue with him and a case could be made for the beginning of the breach with the Baptists prior to the union.

Richardson, Campbell's biographer, said the union in Kentucky had extended itself through most of the western states, resulting in an immense number of converts to the church.[4] This was certainly true in Kentucky as a result of the labors of the evangelists and others, and reports from preachers elsewhere were inundated with glowing reports of baptisms. Garrison and DeGroot recognize this element also, stating, "The story of the union of the Disciples and Christians merges into that of the growth and expansion of the united body in the next decade."[5]

Barton W. Stone, who said, "For 32 years of my ministry I have kept in view the unity of christians as my polar star,"[6] stated near the end of his life, "This union, irrespective of reproach, I view as the noblest act of my life."[7]

John Rogers wrote in his journal that the union

> . . . has accomplished an amount of good which cannot be computed. The importance of that Union has never been appreciated — & perhaps cannot be yet. It will be hereafter, when we, who were the actors in it shall have passed away. It was & is, such a Union as the world never witnessed before nor since. It stands alone in the history of the Church.[8]

SOME LESSONS

This study provides a basis for those who believe in unity of God's people upon the Bible alone to have confidence that it is reasonable and workable. The preachers of a century and a half ago were willing to separate doctrine from opinion and give up preaching on subjects, speculative in nature, that had been argued for years and years without finding a solution in order to allow the Scriptures to be the sole authority. While such a position may sound simplistic, it is a difficult one to achieve unless men are willing to lay aside long held speculations so that the Scriptures can provide the necessary direction. Clarity of Biblical doctrine and concepts can only emerge through the use of correct hermeneutical principles, and speculations and opinions usually stand in the way.

This remarkable achievement of unity is amazing. The people were largely pioneers and the preachers, except for some of the leaders, possessed little formal education for the most part. The key element of their education was the Bible, and as diligent students they sorted out revealed truth from rationalized beliefs. While they did not always lay aside some of the latter, they were unwilling to make them conditions for fellowship.

A second lesson from this noble example is that doctrinal convictions need not be compromised in order to achieve Christian unity. Campbell held no interest in a merger of all the sects with their peculiar doctrines even though some stood against creeds, councils, and division. He viewed his work above those positions, seeking a restoration of the ancient order of things and the ancient gospel. He openly stated his opposition to a merger that would simply mingle concepts together, even though such a union might provide a very honorable alliance.

Neither was Stone willing to compromise doctrine, but would permit others time to study and grow. His position in this regard on the subject of baptism for the remission of sins illustrated this. He recognized that "the people of God have been a long time in the wilderness, and have been misled to the neglect of this ordinance," but that speaking and urging the truth in love, with Christian forbearance, "will ultimately effect what a contrary course will fail to do." He recognized the importance of each persons' soul and believed that people should be given time to learn and accept new concepts instead of leaving them in the wilderness.

Willingness to allow time to throw off old convictions and study and develop new ones stands as one of the major reasons for value of this lesson. Brethren show more concern for an alien sinner still trapped in Egypt than toward an escaped brother who is still in the wilderness. If some of the same kind of patience would be extended toward those who hold some of the same Biblical convictions, much could be done to bring together the Bible-believing segments of our ruptured brotherhood.

The union also demonstrated that people do have the capacity to lay aside long held and cherished opinions when the prayer of Jesus is taken seriously and the goal of world evangelism takes priority. It should surprise no one that when union was accomplished, evangelism flourished. Evangelizing the world stood as their ultimate goal and union served as a major step to achieve it. When world evangelism once more becomes the primary goal of the brotherhood, the prayer of Jesus will again be taken seriously. Human speculation and opinion will remain in the hearts of people and stand as a hindrance to unity when ulterior motives serve as the motivation.

Some brethren see the maintenance of a pure body as their goal. Until world evangelism becomes the goal, it will be difficult for them to put forth any serious effort to accomplish unity. They would see any union as tainting the pureness of body and therefore undesirable. Opinions become as cherished as revealed truth and will often be cherished above the purpose of God to evangelize the world. It is heart-breaking to hear some saints express with deep conviction and genuine sincerity that some "brethren" will not be saved because they have a bus ministry in their church and busses are unscriptural. When maintenance of a pure body is the goal then the tools for carrying out the purpose of God to evangelize the world comes under attack. Such opinions usually become more solidified when held in such an atmosphere and will remain until world evangelism takes precedence over maintenance.

The situation in Ohio illustrated that wrong attitudes foster division. Truth can be handled in such a way that it repels instead of attracts. Threats, intimidation and debates widened the breach. Had the spirit of Stone prevailed in Ohio, a greater union would undoubtedly have occurred.

A final lesson that needs emphasized is that those who were disinterested in unity stooped to name-calling. Terms like "Arians" and "Campbellites" were used to heap abuse upon others. Designations of abuse should have no place in the hearts of those who plea for unity upon the basis of the Bible alone in order to build an atmosphere for world evangelism. It is almost preposterous to think that one who has such a low estimate of his brother that he would heap abuse upon him would have any genuine concern for world evangelism.

The pioneer preachers cherished this accomplishment of union, acclaiming that it stood alone in history. Why does it have to stand alone in history? Why can it not happen again?

---

1. W.T. Moore, pp. 269-270.
2. Williams, p. 417.
3. B.L. Smith, *Alexander Campbell* (St. Louis: The Bethany Press, 1930), p. 171.
4. Richardson, Volume II, p. 395.
5. Garrison and DeGroot, p. 217.
6. Stone, "Notice," *The Christian Messenger,* Volume IX (December, 1835), p. 285.
7. Rogers, *B.W. Stone,* p. 79.
8. "Life and Times of John Rogers," p. 21.

Books

Baxter, William. *Life of Elder Walter Scott.* St. Louis: The Bethany Press, 1926.

Bishop, Robert H. *An Outline of the History of the Church in the State of Kentucky During a Period of Forty Years Containing the Memoirs of Rev. David Rice,* Cincinnati: Art Guild Reprints, Inc., 1824.

Boles, H. Leo. *Biographical Sketches of Gospel Preachers.* Nashville: Gospel Advocate Co., 1932.

Bower, William Clayton. *Central Christian Church, Lexington, Kentucky: A History.* St. Louis: The Bethany Press, 1962.

Braden, Gayle A., and Runyon, Coralie J. *A History of the Christian Church, Maysville, KY.* Lexington: Transylvania Printing Co., 1948.

Bray, John Lester. *John Smith: Pioneer Kentucky Disciple.* Lexington, 1955.

Campbell, Alexander. *Memoirs of Elder Thomas Campbell Together With a Brief Memoir of Mrs. Jane Campbell.* Cincinnati: H.S. Bosworth, 1861.

————. *Schism, Its Bane and Antidote; or the True Foundation of Christian Union.* London: Simpkin & Co. and R. Groombridge; and T. Kirk, 1840.

Cauble, Commodore Wesley. *Disciples of Christ in Indiana: Achievements of a Century.* Indianapolis: Meigs Publishing Company, 1930.

Cleveland, Catherine. *The Great Revival in the West, 1797-1805.* Gloucester: Peter Smith, 1959.

Darst, H. Jackson. *Ante-Bellum Virginia Disciples.* Richmond: Virginia Christian Missionary Society, 1959.

Donan, P. *Memoir of Jacob Creath, Jr.* Cincinnati: R.W. Carroll & Co., 1872.

England, Stephen J. *We Disciples: A Brief View of History and Doctrine.* St. Louis: Christian Board of Publication, 1946.

Evans, Madison. *Biographical Sketches of the Pioneer Preachers of Indiana,* Philadelphia: J. Challen & Sons, 1862.

Fortune, Alonzo Willard. *The Disciples in Kentucky.* Kentucky: The Convention of the Christian Churches, 1932.

Franklin, Joseph, and Headington, J.A. *The Life and Times of Benjamin Franklin.* St. Louis: John Burns, Publisher, 1879.

Freese, J.R. *A History and Advocacy of the Christian Church.* Philadelphia: Christian General Book Concern, n.d. (Around 1848).

Garrison, J.H., ed. *The Reformation of the Nineteenth Century: A Series of Historical Sketches.* St. Louis: Christian Publishing Company, 1901.

Garrison, Winfred Ernest, and DeGroot, Alfred T. *The Disciples of Christ: A History.* St. Louis: The Bethany Press, 1948.

Garrison, Winfred Ernest. *Religion Follows the Frontier: A History of the Disciples of Christ.* New York: Harper & Brothers Publishers, 1931.

Gates, Errett. *The Early Relation and Separation of Baptists and Disciples.* Chicago: The Christian Century Company, 1904.

————. *The Story of the Churches: The Disciples of Christ.* New York: The

Baker & Taylor Co., 1905.

Haley, T.P. *The Dawn of the Reformation: Historical and Biographical Sketches of the Early Churches and Pioneer Preachers of the Christian Church in Missouri.* Kansas City: J.H. Smart & Co., 1888.

Hall, Colby D. *The "New Light Christians:" Initiators of the Nineteenth Century Reformation.* Fort Worth: Stafford-Lowdon Co., 1959.

Harrell, David Edwin, Jr. *Quest for a Christian America: The Disciples of Christ and Amerian Society to 1866.* Volume 1. Nashville: The Disciples of Christ Historical Society, 1966.

Hayden, A.S. *Early History of the Disciples in the Western Reserve, Ohio.* Cincinnati: Chase & Hall, Publishers, 1875.

Haynes, Nathaniel, S. *History of the Disciples of Christ in Illinois, 1819-1914.* Cincinnati: The Standard Publishing Company, 1915.

Hodge, Frederick Arthur. *The Plea and the Pioneers in Virginia.* Richmond: Everett Waddey Company, 1905.

Holland, E.G. *Memoir of Rev. Joseph Badger.* New York: C.S. Francis and Company, 1854.

Hopson, Ella Lord. *Memoirs of Dr. Winthrop Hartly Hopson.* Cincinnati: The Standard Publishing Company, 1887.

Humphreys, E.W. *Memoirs of Deceased Christian Ministers; or, Brief Sketches of the Lives and Labors of 975 Ministers, Who Died Between 1793 and 1880.* Dayton: Christian Publishing Association, 1880.

Jennings, Walter Wilson. *Origin and Early History of the Disciples of Christ.* Cincinnati: The Standard Publishing Company, 1919.

Johnson, Charles A. *The Frontier Camp Meeting: Religion's Harvest Time.* Dallas: Southern Methodist University Press, 1955.

Johnson, L.F. *The History of Franklin County.* Frankfort: Roberts Printing Co., 1912.

Jones, A.D. *Memoir of Elder Abner Jones .* Boston: William Crosby & Company, 1842.

Keith, Noel L. *The Story of D.S. Burnet: Undeserved Obscurity.* St. Louis: The Bethany Press, 1954.

Lamb, Mrs. N.E., corrected and revised by Burnett, J.F. *Autobiography of Abraham Snethen, The Barefoot Preacher.* Dayton: Christian Publishing Association, 1909.

Latourette, Kenneth Scott. *A History of the Expansion of Christianity,* Volume IV. New York: Harper and Brothers Publishers, 1941.

Masters, Frank M. *A History of the Baptists in Kentucky.* Louisville: Kentucky Baptist Historical Society, 1953.

Mathes, James M. *Life of Elijah Goodwin, The Pioneer Preacher.* St. Louis: John Burns, Publisher, 1880.

_____. *Works of Elder B.W. Stone to Which is Added A Few Discourses and Sermons.* Volume I, Cincinnati: Moore, Wilstach, Keys & Co., Printers, 1859.

Meacham, Charles Mayfield. *A History of Christian County of Kentucky*

From Oxcart to Airplane. Nashville: Marshall and Bruce Company, 1930.

Mitchell, Nathan J. *Reminiscences and Incidents in the Life and Travels of a Pioneer Preacher of the "Ancient" Gospel; With a Few Characteristic Discourses.* Cincinnati: Chase and Hall, Publishers, 1877.

Moore, William Thomas. *A Comprehensive History of the Disciples of Christ.* New York: Fleming H. Revell Company, 1909.

Morrill, Milo True. *A History of the Christian Denomination in America, 1794-1911 A.D.* Dayton: The Christian Publishing Association, 1912.

Moseley, J. Edward. *The Disciples of Christ in Georgia.* St. Louis: The Bethany Press, 1954.

Murch, James DeForest. *Christians Only: A History of the Restoration Movement.* Cincinnati: The Standard Publishing Company, 1962.

MacClenny, W.E. *The Life of Rev. James O'Kelly and The Early History of the Christian Church in the South.* Indianapolis: Religious Book Service, 1950.

McKinney, A.L. *Memoir of Elder Isaac N. Walter.* Cincinnati: Rickey, Mallor & Webb, 1857.

Norton, Herman A. *Tennessee Christians.* Nashville: Reed & Company, 1971.

Overman, Neal and Whitaker, O.B. *Overman-Whitaker Debate.* Chicago: M.A. Donohue & Company, 1906.

Peters, George L. *The Disciples of Christ in Missouri.* The Centennial Commission, 1937.

Phillips, William. *Campbellism Exposed; or, Strictures on the Peculiar Tenets of Alexander Campbell.* Cincinnati: Poe and Hitchcock, 1861.

Posey, Walter Brownlow. *The Baptist Church in the Lower Mississippi Valley, 1776-1845.* Lexington: University of Kentucky Press, 1957.

_____. *The Presbyterian Church in the Old Southwest, 1778-1838.* Richmond: John Knox Press, 1952.

Purviance, Levi. *The Biography of Elder David Purviance.* Dayton: B.F. and G.W. Ellis, 1848.

Richards, John Adair. *A History of Bath County.* Yuma, 1961.

Richardson, Robert. *Memoirs of Alexander Campbell.* 2 Vols. Nashville: Gospel Advocate Company, 1956.

Richardson, R. *The Principles and Objects of the Religious Reformation, Urged by A. Campbell and Others.* Bethany: Alexander Campbell, 1853.

Rogers, James R. *The Cane Ridge Meeting House.* Cincinnati: The Standard Publishing Company, 1910.

Rogers, John. *Autobiography of Elder Samuel Rogers.* Cincinnati: The Standard Publishing Company, 1880.

_____. *The Biography of Elder Barton Warren Stone, Written by Himself: With Additions and Reflections.* Fifth Edition. Cincinnati: J.A. & O.P. James, 1847.

_____. *The Biography of Elder J.T. Johnson.* Nashville: Gospel Advocate

Company, 1956.

Russell, Ward. *Church Life in the Blue Grass: 1783-1933.* U.S.A., 1933.

Shaw, Henry K. *Buckeye Disciples: A History of the Disciples of Christ in Ohio.* St. Louis: Christian Board of Publication, 1952.

———. *Hoosier Disciples.* St. Louis: The Bethany Press, 1966.

Smith, Benjamin Lyon. *Alexander Campbell.* St. Louis: The Bethany Press, 1930.

Smith, H.C. *Church History of the North Middletown Community.* Paris, Kentucky: Frank Remington, Printer, 1923.

Spencer, Claude Elbert. *An Author Catalog of Disciples of Christ and Related Groups.* Canton, Missouri: Disciples of Christ Historical Society, 1946.

Spencer, J.H. *A History of Kentucky Baptists From 1769 to 1895.* 2 Vols. Cincinnati: J.R. Baumes, 1885.

Stanford, Belle. *Autobiography and Sermons of Elder Elijah Martindale.* Indianapolis: Carlon and Hollenbeck, Printers, 1892.

Stevenson, Dwight E. *Walter Scott: Voice of the Golden Oracle.* St. Louis: Christian Board of Publication, 1946.

Stone, Barton Warren. *History of the Christian Church in the West.* Reprint from *The Christian Messenger.* Lexington: The College of the Bible, 1956.

Summerbell, J.J. *Quadrennial Book of the American Christian Convention.* Dayton: Christian Publishing Association, 1886.

Summerbell, N., ed. *The Autobiography of Elder Matthew Gardner.* Dayton: Christian Publishing Association, 1874.

———. *A History of the Christian Church from A.M. 4004 to A.D. 1852.* Raleigh, North Carolina: Christian Sun Office, 1852.

Sweet, William Warren. *Religion on the American Frontier: The Baptists, 1783-1830.* Chicago: The University of Chicago Press, 1931.

———. *Religion on the American Frontier: The Presbyterians, 1783-1840.* Volume II. New York: Cooper Square Publishers, Inc., 1964.

———. *Religion in the Development of American Culture, 1765-1840.* New York: Charles Scribner's Sons, 1952.

Thomas, Joseph. *The Life of the Pilgrim, Joseph Thomas.* Winchester, Virginia: J. Foster, Printer, 1817.

VanKirk, Hiram. *The Rise of the Current Reformation.* St. Louis: Christian Publishing Company, 1907.

Vaughan, B.F. *A Centennial History of the Miami, Ohio, Christian Conference, 1819-1919.* Dayton: Christian Publishing Association,

Waldrop, J.W. *History of the Concord Association.* Owenton, Kentucky: News-Herald Print, 1907.

Walker, Dean E. *Adventuring for Christian Unity: A Survey of the History of Churches of Christ (Disciples).* Cincinnati: The Standard Publishing Company, 1935.

(Walsh Relative). *The Life and Times of John Tomline Walsh.* Cincinnati:

BIBLIOGRAPHY

The Standard Publishing Company, 1885.

Ware, Charles Crossfield. *B.W. Stone.* St. Louis: The Bethany Press, 1932.

———. *Kentucky's Fox Creek.* Wilson, North Carolina: Charles Crossfield Ware, 1957.

———. *North Carolina Disciples of Christ.* St. Louis: Christian Board of Publication, 1927.

West, J.W. *Sketches of Our Mountain Pioneers.* Lynchburg, Virginia: J.W. West, 1939.

West, William Garrett. *Barton Warren Stone: Early American Advocate of Christian Unity.* Nashville: The Disciples of Christ Historical Society, 1954.

Whitsitt, William H. *Origin of the Disciples of Christ (Campbellites).* Louisville: Baptist Book Concern, 1891.

Wilcox, John Augustus. *Life of Elder John Smith.* Nashville: G.A. Company, 1956.

Yancey, Mrs. Robert M. *Disciples of Christ At May's Lick, Kentucky.* (Centennial Publication), 1941.

Periodicals

Badger, Joseph, *Christian Palladium* (Union Mills, N.Y.), 1832-1839.

Burnet, D.S. *The Evangelical Enquirer* (Dayton), 1830-1831.

Campbell, Alexander. *The Christian Baptist,* 1823-1830.

———. *The Millennial Harbinger,* 1830-1842.

Johnson, John T. and Hall, B.F. *Gospel Advocate,* 1835-1836.

Scott, Walter. *The Evangelist,* 1832-1842.

Stone, Barton W. *The Christian Messenger,* 1826-1836, 1840-1844.

Pamphlets and Booklets

Burnett, J.F. "The Origin and Principles of the Christians," Booklet 1. (Dayton).

———. "Rev. James O'Kelly: A Champion of Religious Liberty," Booklet 2. (Dayton).

———. "Rev. Abner Jones: The Man Who Believed and Served," Booklet 3. (Dayton).

———. "Rev. Barton Warren Stone: The Man Who Studied and Taught," Booklet 4. (Dayton).

———. "Elias Smith: Reformer, Preacher, Journalist, Doctor; and "Horace Mann: Christian Statesman and Educator," Booklet 5. (Dayton).

———. "Rev. B.W. Stone: Did He Join the Disciples of Christ?" Booklet 6. (Dayton).

Campbell, Thomas. *The Declaration and Address.* Birmingham: The Berean Press, 1951.

Lee, Walter M. *A History of the Elkhorn Baptists Association.* A small unnumbered booklet.

Unpublished Material

Gano, John Allen. "John Allen Gano's Biographical Notebook, December, 1831-1861." (Typewritten copy).

Grant, J.W. "A Sketch of the Reformation in Tennessee," (Typewritten copy). Unpublished manuscript in Disciples Historical Society, Nashville.

Rogers, John. "Life and Times of John Rogers, of Carlisle, Kentucky." (Microfilm). Southern Historical Collection. Chapel Hill.

Index